I0500191

CO-OPVERTISING™

A MOVEMENT TO RE-DEFINE YOUR
SUCCESS
BY SIMPLY HELPING OTHERS FIRST!

JEFF LEVIN

CO-OPVERTISING™
A MOVEMENT TO RE-DEFINE YOUR SUCCESS BY SIMPLY HELPING
OTHERS FIRST!

Copyright © 2017 by Jeff Levin & Leverage Enterprises, Inc.

All Rights Reserved. No part of this book may be reproduced,
transmitted, distributed in any form, by any means, electronic,
photocopying, recording, scanning, or otherwise, without written
permission from the author.

ISBN-13: 978-1546460473

Requests should be addressed to:
Leverage Enterprises, Inc.

10769 Broadway
No. 214
Crown Point, IN 46307
866.217.8425

www.jefflevin.com
www.Co-Opvertisingnetwork.com
www.co-opmovement.com
www.levelupmybiz.com

"TO ACHIEVE MASSIVE SUCCESS, YOU MUST BE WILLING TO SERVE THE MASSES FIRST."
-JEFF LEVIN

CONTENTS

i   PRAISES   i

INTRODUCTION   1

1   RE-DEFINING YOUR SUCCESS   3

2   DISCOVERING YOUR MISSION   12

3   BECOMING A LEADER   35

4   GETTING THE MOST FROM NETWORKING   40

5   CREATING VALUABLE CO-OPVERTISING™ OFFERS   49

6   EXECUTING CO-OPVERTISING™ DEALS   59

7   50X YOUR PROMOTIONAL POWER   65

8   BUILDING ACTIVE STRATEGIC ALLIANCES   68

9   TRACKING YOUR PROGRESS   81

10   LEVELING UP YOUR BUSINESS   84

11   JOINING THE CO-OPVERTISING™ MOVEMENT   90

ABOUT THE AUTHOR   93

APPENDIX A: CO-OPVERTISING™ EXAMPLES   95

APPENDIX B: CO-OPVERTISING™ TRACKER   102

PRAISES FOR THE CO-OPVERTISING™ MOVEMENT

"Being on mission is the foundation of every business. However, many small business owners have a hard time living their mission due to the everyday grind of running a business & working hard to earn a living. The Co-Opvertising™ Movement helps entrepreneurs find purpose, build a network and grow their business by simply helping others first. Jeff has done an amazing job creating a platform to do just that." – Melanie Jane Nicolas, America's Leading Authority in Raising Wealthy Kids.

" Having participated in many different business networking groups and events over the last two decades in doing business, I have found no other group like the Co-Opvertising™ Network. The members are truly vested in wanting to help you succeed. Networking will never be the same once attending a Co-Op Movement Event. The founders, Jeff and Lisa Levin are two beautiful spirits that totally give their all to their members in helping them succeed. As a result, not only am I a member, but I am also the Movement Leader for the Chicago Metro Region. The Co-Op Rocks!" - Wendy Lee, Exit Realty Broker

"Jeff Levin is the kind of leader who I believe leads with heart, common sense, and the will to make change happen for a community of people through his passion and talent in making relationships happen. He knows the power good relationships can bring, and supplies the motivation and resources that can turn opportunities that not only can grow business, but also provide the platform to give businesses the chance to reach a high-level victory that they deserve. Jeff is one valuable resource you want in your tribe." – Anita Meyers, InnerScope Consulting

"Jeff is a leader you would want in your circle of 5. The level of leadership in a person is not measured by what they say but what they do and I have watched Jeff bring a mass amount of people together for common good, I have watched Jeff build for events with standing room only, I have watched Jeff attract some of the most sought out public figures (multi-millionaires) to his events. His focus on serving others and helping people "up their game" is contagious and has helped MANY people from many different professions." - Andreas Papakostas, Global Entrepreneur

"Jeff's unique ability to understand business and help put together business strategies has helped me by leveling up my business. His theory of putting others first and leading with your mission has really opened doors for me and hundreds more that participate in the movement." – Bob Lockwood, Creative Producer – Full Armour Studios

"Jeff Levin is amazing! The insight he was able to share was a great AHHH HHAAAA moment. I am so excited to start stepping in the right direction. Thank you! Entrepreneurs succeeding by helping others first – right on point! I urge all of you to invest in an opportunity to meet with Jeff. He provide a new insight that after 10 years of doing business, makes me feel like it's my first day! New ideas, goals and excitement is back on my business plan." – Mary Ziola-Vega, Epic United Recruiting

"I love the Co-Opvertising™ way of doing business that Jeff Levin promotes. It teaches entrepreneurs the importance of looking to help others first and trusting that when we do that we will have more business than we could ever know what to do with. I recommend Jeff's LevelUp program because it focuses on purpose, passion and positivity which are all highly connected to achieving success." – Jen Coffel, Best Selling Author, Business Coach and Co-Founder of Handing Hope

"When I decided to attend my first Co-Op Movement Live Event, I had no idea what the driving force was behind this amazing network. Jeff and Lisa's mission of helping others first and serving community was completely in line with my beliefs. They are so dedicated to helping businesses thrive and showing them how to do this through helping others FIRST! For these reasons, I could not wait to share these events in my own community and am launching the Chicago South Suburbs Group. A movement of this kind should not be contained to one area. There are so many businesses and communities that can benefit from this Movement!" - Ruth Kutschke, Owner The Planning Place Events

"Being in sales and business, networking is a part of what I do. The majority of organized networking events are a little bit different but much of the same. When I was introduced to the Co-Op Movement, I loved the concept of giving and establishing relationships first, before asking for business. If we as a business community wrap our heads around this concept and truly unite, the possibilities would be endless. I was so inspired by Jeff and Lisa's Mission that I asked to be a part of their expansion into the Schaumburg area. I am grateful to be a part of the Co-Op team." – Majid Zafer, Entrepreneur

INTRODUCTION

Co-Opvertising™ began as a strategy back in 2008 but little did we know that this strategy would be a movement capable of re-defining success, but it very well is and we would like to share it with the world. Those who have succeeded in anything in life have always done it by finding ways to work together with people that shared common missions and goals. It is also apparent, that those who have succeeded big always had a big problem to solve and were driven to find a solution to impact lives. They rarely if ever achieved success alone. They always had people right by their side. We invented Co-Opvertising™ as a gift to the Entrepreneurs of the world to provide them with a way to leverage their extremely valuable relationship capital they've acquired through networking and customer service to grow their businesses at minimal costs. A gift that is completely untouchable without adopting one slight but powerful shift in traditional business philosophy – a willingness to help others first! This fundamental shift in thought process is the key to success for entrepreneurs. In fact, it is impossible to see the benefits of growth beyond self unless you can see others involved in helping achieve your goals, which is why most companies never grow beyond themselves and find themselves struggling to get by. The concept of Co-Opvertising™ is the key to success because it requires you to grow through others and it requires you to build a team the only way possible, through accelerated trust building practices we've perfected over the past fourteen years. It also requires you to be a giving person first without any expectation for gain and in this book we show you just how powerful this can be for your company. Best of all, when companies are working together everybody wins, including the companies involved, customers and the communities. A total win.win.win!

Imagine a country where companies were driven to help others first and work together for the common good of others they serve in their businesses and in the community. Imagine if they had a purpose far greater than their profits. You may not be able to picture this, but we have seen gathering more than 3000 people already just in the Chicagoland area that are doing just that and the energy when we gather at our Co-Opvertising™ Movement Live Events is infectious enough to believe that, this strategy has become a movement to create purpose driven leaders across this country that are capable of impacting lives in ways we've yet to see. All from a simple concept – to help others first! We hope you will join us as we re-define success across the country! Enjoy the book and if it inspires you, share it!

CHAPTER ONE

RE-DEFINING YOUR SUCCESS

·······························

"You only succeed when you are willing to help others first." –
Jeff Levin

Success can be defined in many ways, but I believe that you only
succeed when you are willing to help enough others succeed
first! Only then will you reap the true rewards. So, we have set
out to inspire a new sense of collaboration in business, one
which gets to trusting, sustainable relationships quickly & puts
those new relationships into action!

It is our mission to help re-write the purpose and LevelUp the
mission of each and every company to inspire them to have a
purpose for their profitability in business! We believe and have
proven time and time again, that when you lead with a purpose
or mission that is far greater than your business and yourself,
your business will follow, grow and prosper in ways you could
never have dreamed of before. After all, your company and

every company is there to serve people within their communities. When you are willing serve the masses first, you will become massively successful in whatever you do.

If every company across the United States and beyond adds purpose to their profits, they are making their cause a priority in their companies. This means, their values and motivation will shift to achieve what they set out to achieve, using their profitability and influence to fuel both impact and outcome.

Let's talk about the impact a simple but profound shift in the Mission of a company can have on their communities and collectively across the nation.

1. **Instantly positions a company for growth and community leadership**

Years ago, I brought on a client as a coach that happened to be in the sign industry. For those who are unaware, the sign business is very competitive and very tough to differentiate your business on anything but price. However, when I began to work with this client, I noticed he had a 50 foot windmill in his backyard and had a real passion for clean energy. Now, up until this point, this client had been in business for almost 20 years. He had some passion but was quite drained from a business perspective, but my hiring couldn't have come at a better time, because after just a few sessions, I asked this key question: What if you re-branded your company around your passion and led with it? What do you mean, he asked? Well it isn't normal to have a 50 foot windmill in the backyard, right? Why do you have that? Then he proceeded to verbally re-focus his entire purpose for his business. He said with passion, "Because it is his goal to power his company through clean energy!" And, it was his mission to have the entire region he lived and operated within to be powered by clean energy as well! Wow! He went from an ordinary sign company, to now an advocate for clean energy. His products now carried environmental benefits and because he was now advocating for the community, he no longer had to compete on price to win clients! He became so excited to re-brand and began to lead with his mission in contacting developers, builders and realtors – the companies he had always struggled to win business from for the past 20 years. Now, not only did they want to give him their sign business for new developments, but they even offered to donate a plot of land for the windmill in the subdivisions they were developing and building. All because he led with his mission. So, by adding a purpose to his business, he was able to establish new relationships with major alliances that were very difficult to arrange in the past. He was also able to become a community advocate & became profitable from all of the new bulk business that came from the newly formed alliances. This can happen with your company and every other company in this country and it is our mission to ignite the spark that inspires you to find your purpose and use it to make a difference, grow your business & inspire others around you to do the same.

Impacting lives

I prefer the term Entrepreneur rather than small business owner because an entrepreneur sets out to grow and capitalize on opportunities. Companies become small business owners when they fail to include a vision large enough and a mission strong enough to serve the masses. When you add a mission that adds purpose for your profits, you become impactful. Your company values instantly are defined or re-aligned to enable your company to fulfill its mission. When this happens, you will begin to impact the lives of everyone that interacts with your business. You will attract the greatest of people to come work for you because their job will now serve a greater purpose than just making money because after all, everyone desires a career that is meaningful and impactful. Plus, your clients will want to help you more with referrals and more business because of your purpose. As a result, your business will begin to catch fire and grow more rapidly, because you now have a purpose for your profits! You lead with your purpose or mission and your business follows! We believe every company not only has the ability but also the responsibility to be impactful to the lives they serve in business. Those who take that responsibility are the ones who go on to be massively successful.

Impacting the US

Imagine every company in the United States leading with a strong, impactful mission? All 28 million entrepreneurs! When I do, I get excited! Here's why: as a business owner, you are a leader, whether you accept or not! When you put yourself out there and lead with your mission, there are now others at stake besides you, besides your family and besides your employees. This means that you are responsible for the success of others, not just yourself in business. Your mission will become your biggest reason you will fight through the challenges, because now you cannot quit, in fact, you must succeed, because there are so many others that now depend on your success! So, whether you have one employee or are self-employed, with a mission far greater than yourself or your business, you have taken the first key step toward becoming a true leader – a key ingredient to being highly successful in anything you do, especially in business. This will allow you to attract the right people into your life who are needed to help you carry out your mission, the instant you put yourself out there. It's amazing how much your business and your life changes when you begin to share your purpose. You are an inspiration and a true leader waiting to happen and people that you were born and meant to serve are waiting for you to step up and serve at a whole new level.

Plus, aside from the benefits of positioning a company for rapid growth, when you make your mission about serving the masses, you set an example for your employees, strategic business alliances, clients and the communities you serve. The values you establish, your actions and influence in the community will set the example on how leaders should serve. When our leaders set the right example and get results, people will follow in due time. If you are reading this, I'll bet you didn't realize that when you decided to go into business, you were going to impact and change lives to this magnitude? But you can! You can and you will have a tremendous impact, when you make the decision to make your business about the others that you were meant to serve, deep inside your heart.

When you make the decision to lead with a purpose greater than yourself, you put us one step closer to re-defining success in the business community across this country. We want to create companies of impact and purpose all across America. For one simple, but profounding reason: when every company across the US goes on mission to impact, it will not only accelerate the growth of your companies but it will have a long lasting impact in the people our companies serve and support. Being mission-driven, will shift company values to more closely align with the true purpose of a business – to solve a problem in the community or within the population of people they serve. They are not there solely to make the owners rich. They are there to serve a purpose & when they fulfill that purpose, both you and your company will prosper.

We are at a point in time in our country, where leaving problems for our leaders to fix is no longer a viable solution to our problems in this country. I believe that most of the problems that occur within a town, city, region, state or country can be fixed when companies take their responsibility and do their part as community leaders, not just business owners. In a capitalist society, as a business owner, you have decided to partner in the success of this country. Part of that success, includes creating thriving companies that employs people. When people are employed – they are productive citizens. When they are not employed, they are usually destructive. When you have a greater purpose for the profitability of your company, you place yourself and your company in a position to dramatically impact communities and impact lives.

Adding a genuine purpose to the success of your company will not only allow your company to grow and employ people, but it will literally change their lives. Ponder this for a moment: People spending most of their waking lives working in companies they do not own. Most of their days are spent with you building and operating your companies. That is an incredible blessing to you. Now think about this – most people hate their jobs and dread getting up for work each day, regardless if they are getting paid or not. I would venture to say that if you are reading this book, you have left a company because you could not invest one more minute in an environment that didn't serve you in a positive way? I know, because I was that person too. People do want to get paid, but they also want to spend their lives in an environment that is meaningful and add value to their lives and others. They yearn for something more – just like you did, right? As an entrepreneur it is your duty to be on mission for something more, so that you can provide an opportunity for others to have meaning in their lives, by serving as employees in your company. Everyone is not capable of starting something, but everyone is capable of living a fulfilling life. It is your job to first create a mission that inspires you, to inspire others and create the environment that people cannot wait to get up every day and serve. When your business is about something more than you and something more than your business, people will be excited to work for you and align with you to carry out your mission. What's exciting about this, is now you are setting a positive example for the families of the people serving your company. They will take those values home to their families within the community and be inspired to make a difference themselves because of what you taught them in your company – where they spend most of their waking hours each and every week! There is a real opportunity right now in this country to re-establish what it means to be successful in business and we believe that by Leveling Up your mission, we can get there! I firmly believe that creating a positive environment around serving others can solve most of the problems we have in our communities. You can't hate people when you are focused on helping them. When people are impacting lives of others, they realize that true success is not about the money they are earning. It's about using your skills and talents to make a real difference and when we help enough others with those talents, you are rewarded financially, spiritually, relationally and physically. Unfortunately, poor examples in leadership has lead people to believe otherwise and it's time that we get back to basics in this country and I believe that there is no better place to begin than with the Entrepreneurs – the most influential and driven people in this country.

Timing is everything too! An entire generation is coming into the workforce now that are highly connected, highly educated and greatly concerned about how they spend their time. They want to have impact. They are not interested in earning just a paycheck. Will you create a company that attracts the next generation or will you miss out on this opportunity? You will if you LevelUp Your Mission. You will if decide to make your company and success about something more than padding your own personal pockets and instead, make it about serving others. Serving a massive amount of others through both your products and services. Do you believe you were meant to serve the masses? Well you are! God created us all with gifts and experiences that can benefit the masses in a positive way and your company can be the vehicle to reaching and serving the people you were meant to reach! How exciting is that?

It is our goal, through this mission, to re-define what success means to you and every other Entrepreneur across this country and create an environment that gives you the support and confidence to continue moving forward and to never, ever give up, no matter how hard it gets. Because this journey is not about you – it's really about the people you serve.

It is my hope for you that after reading this book, you will be inspired by a new-found purpose to have an impact on those around you through your business and be excited to re-write your mission statement and begin proclaiming it to every person you meet and speak with. There are close to 28 million Entrepreneurs in the small business community across the USA that employ the largest segment of our population. We can make a difference, one business at a time & together we can create a new definition of success that creates long-lasting positive impact in communities across the US. It's time to stop waiting for the government, politicians and big business to fix issues that as leaders in the business community can fix. The future of our country, our children, our families are depending on us!

As you read this book and become inspired to re-define your success, we want to hear about it! Share your newfound purpose for your profits in your local Co-Opvertising™ Network Facebook Group with the hashtag #mission28M and go to www.co-opmovement.com to submit your mission today! We need your help in reaching Entrepreneurs in your community too! So please invite them to join our online Co-Opvertising™ Network groups on Facebook or visit an upcoming Co-Op Movement Live Event in your area. All upcoming events are listed online and can be found by going to www.Co-Opvertisingnetwork.com.

CHAPTER TWO

DISCOVERING YOUR MISSION

....

"No man or woman is meant to serve in a small capacity" - Jeff
Levin

In order to help you determine what your purpose or mission is
in business, let me share with you how we discovered ours. I
believe that God has blessed us all with gifts to share with the
world. Our life's experiences, both good and bad are meant to
help us find just what they are and how they can be used to
change and impact lives. I believe that no man or woman was
meant to serve in a small capacity. We were all given the tools
to impact the masses, but God also gave us the FREE will to
decide to take the appropriate actions to unleash the power
within you that is only found when you align your life's work,
with your true gifts and talents. In fact, by not choosing to
recognize your gifts, your life is still used for others to use as

examples of what not to do. Either way you look at it, your life was meant to impact lives for the better. The question is, what path, what example will you choose? Will you be a positive or negative impact? Either way, it will require your willingness to find your gifts and then have the faith to pursue the path that you were called to journey.

I wasn't born with the wisdom I have today, in fact, like everyone else, I've acquired the vast amount of my wisdom through major life changing experiences that have altered both my values and life purpose. In order for you to appreciate the man I am today and how I discovered meaning and purpose in my life, let me share with you my life's amazing journey.

I grew up in a low to middle class household. My Dad was a hard-working steel worker and my mom a housewife. They were married straight out of high school and shortly after I was born. If there's one thing for certain, I was taught by my parents that you could have anything you wanted in life if you were willing to work hard to get it. My parents were great examples of that. They didn't have the education or the support of parents having lost their parents at an early age, but they made up for it in work ethic, attitude and drive that took my Dad from sweeping floors to the executive offices in the largest steel company in the country.

That work ethic and competitive attitude was definitely passed down to us. From the time I can remember, I have always wanted to be the best and win at everything I did. Spelling bees, flash card competitions in elementary school, even beating someone to the car after school. I have always wanted to be the best because I loved standing out and how it made me feel. That drive helped me accel academically, athletically and professionally. I truly believed there wasn't anything I couldn't achieve.

I was the first to not only go to college in my family but to also get an athletic scholarship. I will admit, coming out of high school, the only thing I wanted to do is become a professional baseball player and I got my chance in 1992 when I signed to attend Carthage College. I didn't care about my major, I just wanted to play baseball. However, I didn't make it more than 1 year there because I did something that I vowed to never, ever do again in my life – I gave up. You see, I was a great left-handed pitcher, but I was being overlooked and did not trust why God put me in that position and how I was being molded. I did not know God at the time, so it felt like, there was no hope so why continue. I was being overlooked, so what was the point? So instead of buckling down and working hard to prove myself, I decided to end my career in baseball and transfer to Purdue to study Electrical Engineering, because that would allow me to get a good paying job. Boy was that a tough decision, but a huge life lesson looking back. I didn't want to put in the work. I was a star in high school, so I expected it to be easier, but instead the opposite occurred and through adversity, I gave up instead of doing what I tell people each and every day of my life – to never, ever give up. Because staying in the game is 95% of the battle.

I went on to study Engineering at Purdue and graduated with honors. I went on to work as an Engineering Project Manager at the largest steel company in the United States. I ran major manufacturing line electrical automation upgrades for nearly 8 years and through the process, I went back to school to get my M.B.A. from Loyola University Chicago. Prior to attending grad school, nothing really clicked for me. I was smart enough to be an engineer, but it wasn't my passion. I did it because it was difficult and would increase my chances of making a decent living, but I just never fit into that world. I was an outgoing person that was fascinated with people, which is polar opposite of engineers as you may already know. While attending grad school, I discovered what I really liked to do – build businesses. I absolutely fell in love with entrepreneurship. I knew it was what I wanted to do, but didn't know what or how that would happen.

2001 started off great! I graduated with my M.B.A. and married my wife Lisa, the most wonderful person in the world, who I've been married to for over 16 years. I got a significant raise at work and was finally seeing the fruits of my labor. Life was good. Then later that year in the fall, I was running for the phone at home, because at the time we still had phones connected to the wall. As I approached the phone, my knees buckled and I fell to the ground. I thought that was weird, and thought very little about it. Then it happened again, while outside playing catch with the football. In addition to issues with my reflexes, my hands and feet began to feel tingly. I went to the doctor to discover, I had the beginning stages of Gillian Barre Syndrome, which was an autoimmune disease that attacks the nerves in the body. The tingly sensation was like my nerves short circuiting and that sensation found it's way all the way up my entire body. It got to the point where I could not walk any longer, I could only drink thick drinks because I would choke on my fluids because the flapper in my throat was not working properly either. It was very scary, but I will say this – I always knew I would be ok. I think it was because so many people were praying for us and so many people were coming by every day to pray over me and help. I was not a Godly person at the time but during life and death circumstances, I think people become open to just about anything and being a stubborn person, it was probably the only way to open my mind to what was happening in my life. God was heavily present and I didn't know it at the time, but he was saving my life. One evening the tingling was so bad that I couldn't sleep, so I got up and struggled to walk into the living room by holding onto the walls, because I could barely walk. As I laid on the couch, I remember crying out for help. Something overcame me (which later I learned was God). The words I cried were more like a plead for help. I was not willing to give up, but I knew I could not do it on my own any longer! And, thankfully, with God, waiting for me to finally surrender, he gave me the help I needed to overcome this devastating condition! For those who follow Christ, you have probably had a similar experience, but if you were like me before, you would say, this guy is nuts! I respect your opinion, however, I believe that without accepting Christ that night into my life, I would not be here to help you!

The next day was truly a new day. The symptoms began to subside & within a few weeks I was no longer choking on my food or drinks from my organs shutting down & the numbness that began in my feet and worked it's way up to my neck, had completely subsided. Recovery didn't stop there with me having to relearn how to walk again, but I cannot tell you how grateful I was to be back in the game & have a shot at life once again!

After returning to work, things just weren't the same. I was grateful for still having a job, after having been out of work for 3 months, but I wanted to do something more. Something that had real, long lasting impact, but didn't know what that was. I was always a leader on the field playing sports, in the workplace and in my family – the one you could count on to deliver when times got tough, so I wanted to find a way to INSPIRE, IMPACT and IMPROVE people's lives with that same gifts. I wanted to use my experience, which most would consider to be devastating, to show people in hopeless situations that there is hope and to never, ever give up because I truly believe that your challenges in life are your greatest blessings – they are a part of God's plan to get people to turn to him & when you do, circumstances change – just like mine! Life doesn't happen to you, it happens for you to realize what you are here for. If you are somebody searching for your why, or meaning in your life or business, look at the challenges you've overcome. The opportunities lie within those challenges, because unless you are dead, your story can impact and change lives if you let it. This story can be told as either a Victor or a Victim, that is entirely up to how you choose to see your experiences in life. But, as long as you are living, you are succeeding, the question is do you see that? Have you acknowledged the learnings? Did you choose to do things differently? The answers to those questions will determine whether you move forward or not in life!

Shortly after recovering, I was contacted by a business coaching franchise opportunity. I never knew such a profession existed but it definitely intrigued me. As I mentioned, I was an athlete and my coaches were very influential in my life, so it sounded very interesting to me. I was a year out of MBA school and so helping people grow businesses sounded very interesting to me as well, so I began to pursue the opportunity. Two weeks later, I made the biggest investment in my life and became the owner of a business coaching franchise with Action International Business Coaching (now ActionCoach). I went all in. We were not independently wealthy so we had to mortgage the house and take out lines of credit to pay for the franchise and the start-up, but this gave me an opportunity to get into a more meaningful role doing what I'm great at – motivating people and building business.

I did well from the beginning. In the first 2 years, I was one of the top grossing coaches in the franchise, but something wasn't right for me with the model. I was attracting companies that were smaller and I think it was because being the Engineer that I was, I enjoyed building companies much more than helping a larger company get better. I was naturally attracted to people that were starting off. I did well, kept clients for years, and even grew a few companies to the point they were able to franchise and expand, but I began to struggle with the business model and that made it difficult for me to follow the model given to me by the franchise. So I began looking for solutions outside of the coaching world that would enable me to serve the market that I felt I could serve best and that needed me the most.

In 2007, I came up with a concept called Co-Opvertising™ and began the development of a system called GrowthPOD.com, where companies like yours can Co-Opvertise and grow together. The system enabled people to cross market to each other's email databases, which was quite revolutionary at the time, without social media. This system took several years and thousands of dollars to develop. I became immersed into GrowthPOD.com and the only way to rid myself of my obligations to the franchise was to file bankruptcy, so we did that in 2008. This led to a series of large changes in our life that included going back to the work in the corporate world to allow us to get back on our feet financially and also pay for the development of our system, which I knew, some way, shape or form would be awesome for small business owners.

It was heartbreaking to have to go back to work. At times I felt like such a failure, because we were starting all over again as a family, without anything really to show for it. The decision actually moved us across the country to the East Coast where I had the opportunity to serve in Corporate Management at a large, regulated energy company, building their Nuclear Project Management Program for their fleet of nuclear plants. I had worked in corporate before, when I began my career, but neither my coaching business or my previous experience in the steel industry could prepare me for what I was about to experience while working in Energy. It was the most chaotic, cut throat and political company I have ever worked for in my life. There wasn't a day that went by that I wasn't afraid of losing my job. In 4 years, I went through 4 mergers or reorganizations, all of which put my job in danger, but there was a saving grace in this entire experience that only God could have his hands on & it worked perfectly of course. We lived in Maryland, around 12 hours from any of our closest family members. Both Lisa and I grew up very close to our families so up until that point, it was difficult to become a family of our own. So this move gave us the opportunity to become a family of our own. Lisa came from a strong Christian family and knew to seek council from God and give him control. I on the other hand, did not but with the challenges we had recently faced with our finances and being far away from our families, it made sense to find a church locally and dig in. We began attending Bay Area Community Church and for some reason, this time, we were ready to dive in and seek the wisdom he had to offer. This decision changed our lives. It gave us new hope. It helped us understand that no man that enters this earth is perfect and our greatest gifts are those we experience as trials in our lives. So, this decision helped us get back on our feet as a family and as a result, we became a praying family and we luckily began to see the blessings happening around us every single day – even the challenges that most people would see in our situation – we began to thank God for the challenges because even though they took us far away from our family, they brought us back into God's family and what an honor that was! It was so much of a blessing that I became obsessed with sharing the impact it was having on my life with everyone I knew – including those at work.

In 2010, the company I was working for in Maryland, was acquired by the largest Energy company in the country. The headquarters was located in Chicago and since I worked for

Corporate, it was either go back to Chicago or lose my job. So since the system we were building was not quite ready, we decided to take the opportunity to move back home, closer to family and take the position.

After 2 years of working through the merger in Chicago, and dealing with major conflicts with the new company culture, I decided it was time to come back into the business and grow GrowthPOD.com.

At no point in time, after going through the many challenges we faced, did I ever even think to quit or give up. That has never been an option, because I truly belief that life's opportunities are found inside of our challenges. So I didn't want to miss out. Plus I knew that we had a great way to help companies grow.

So I entered back into the business and it began to grow. We grew our client base in GrowthPOD.com that was greater than we've even done, but then we plateaued and could not get over the hump. We weren't make enough money and Lisa and I were having trouble working together. I was done. For the second time in my life, I was ready to give up and go back to corporate. I began to seek interview opportunities. I interviewed with a company that I really like and got all the way to the end to find out that I was not chosen for the job. Later I found that they decided to go with someone that sat across from me at my previous job in Chicago. What a blow but this lit a fire in me. I treated this as a sign, that maybe I should stick around in the business and make it work, because I felt like there was no choice. I was running out of money and didn't know what else to do, so I decided to stay in the business, but do things a bit differently. So I created an online network that was on mission to teach companies the success principles we built into the usage of GrowthPOD.com. In order to effectively use any referral strategy, you have to build trust with others first and do it quickly. So I created a Facebook group called the Chicagoland Co-Opvertising™ Network that was on a mission to help others first, because if you want others to promote your business, you have to promote or help them first. We quickly grew to over 2500 members after around 1.5 years and began hosting events with hundreds of people, because people loved what we were about and what we do. I knew right then, that I was meant to be in this business and even though it was tough, we had to push through because what we had was a concept that thousands of others wanted. From there, we thought to ourselves, well what would happen if we had access to all 28 million entrepreneurs across the country? What would be the impact of every business matched the culture of the Co-Opvertising™ Movement? It would be incredible. So I set out on a mission to create the tools and environment to reach businesses with a simple, yet profound new way of doing business. You only succeed when you are willing to help enough others succeed first! This simple concept can change companies, communities and lives and I want to share this concept with every single business owner across the United States.

Success Re-Defined:

Help Others. Grow Your Business. Serve Community. Give Back!

I'm a firm believer that most of the problems we experience in our country are directly related to employment or lack there of. People invest most of their waking hours working for companies. If we as business owners are committed to creating companies of purpose, it will inspire the people associated with our companies to structure their lives around helping others too. As entrepreneurs, you have an outright obligation to grow your company. You are a leader in your own mind and right, but you are not until you have others following you. What example will you set, so others will follow? Imagine if your goal was to impact lives with your profits? As a part of the Co-Op Movement, you have committed to becoming massively successful by serving the masses first!

If you know people that are looking to have an impact or are extremely impactful & influential people, we would love to meet them and share their stories. Join us by going to **www.co-opmovement.com** now! We are looking for contacts in every major metropolitan city across the US to help us inspire people to have purpose for their profits and help us re-define success, by simply helping others first!

What started as my quest to teach business owners a new strategy to grow their business, using a system that I worked hard to developed, has turned into a movement that can and will impact the masses, just by offering an alternative definition of success. Does it match my vision exactly from what it was when I began designing GrowthPOD.com? No, not by far and here's why. When I began developing the program, I thought to myself, I just came up with a billion dollar idea. I was thinking strictly of the benefits I would attain and what I could do with those benefits for myself. It took nearly losing everything again to realize that this business and my gifts were not for me at all and that it was my duty to do whatever it took get the message out and show people just how powerful having a purpose is in business and in life and that if you listen and follow God's plan and you do it for him, not for yourself, amazing things happen that you just cannot explain, other than, it's not about me. This life folks; your gifts and abilities are not about you. They are yours, but you are designed and placed into situations where you must share them with the world and when you do, amazing things happen. I am here to tell you that going through an illness, losing everything I owned through bankruptcy, going through the challenges I faced each and every day in Corporate America fighting for my job daily and nearly losing it all again, was worth every single bit of it and more, because it is exactly what was needed for me to die to my own needs and trust God with why he put me here and what my job was to do. My challenges have been my greatest gifts in life coupled with my strong faith, which was another by-product of going through the trials we've faced over the years. My faith taught me that I didn't have to be in control and that God would never give me more than I could handle. I learned that after reading the Bible, the greatest success book on the planet. I've only given up once in life and that was on my baseball career, which is nothing compared to the people that we read about every day that choose to give up on their lives or cannot deal with the uncertainty of the future. If they only decided to take one more step or learned to ask God for wisdom in why they were placed in the challenging circumstance they were in. Maybe they would see the lesson and come out on the other end and become an influence and teacher to empower others struggling with the same situation. Folks, the opposite of fear is faith and when I first went into business, I had a ton of fear and very little to no faith, but after going through the trials and finding my faith in God, I have rid myself of any fear or doubt that no matter what, I was put on this earth to give people hope and to never, ever give up. God doesn't make junk and no person or cause is disposable as long as you have the faith to get through the challenges and what I want to do is help you see where you are needed, help you develop a purpose for your company that serves the area of the population where you can have the greatest impact and provide you with the support and the environment to grow, develop and to never give up! Plus with a strong purpose, you really can't give up because there are too many people counting on you to come through!

Discovering Your Purpose

So, now that you've made the commitment to join the www.co-opmovement.com, it's time to put you and your business into motion! When things are moving, momentum happens! Momentum is the key to impact and impact is what drives results! So, I hope after hearing my mission and story, I have stirred up enough in you to want to pursue your true calling and purpose. I am confident that it's the only way to unlock your true potential and I look forward to hearing more about it! Feel free to join us on Facebook or Follow us on Twitter to share your newfound purpose! There's something to be said about publicly proclaiming your mission and then asking for people to help! Try it – we have the perfect environment for you to share, since we all share a common vision.

As an entrepreneur, you know your number one purpose is to generate revenue for your business, which will most likely be used to provide for your family. That is always the core motivation, or at least that was the case for me! But, let me tell you why knowing your true purpose is so important after making a decision to build and grow your dream business. Because, it takes you out of the equation and prevents you from giving up, because there is far more at stake than simply your income and your family. There are masses of people that are depending upon you and your solution to improve their lives through your products and services and you must find a way to fulfill those needs. When you have a purpose, it replaces your own needs and puts the entire focus on helping others first, which Is what the Co-Op Movement is all about. Remember, when you help enough others succeed, you will too! Adding a purpose or as I call it, a mission, is like a written guarantee for success. Now, will it be easy now that you have a mission? – NO! Because, just by identifying the meaning behind your company, and expanding your vision around what it will really look like to serve the people that need you the most, you will still undergo many challenges along the way! That should be expected & quite frankly, welcomed. Because, by accepting your calling or mission, you have accepted the responsibility of becoming the person or as I like to say, leader you were intended to be. Your learning curve is your life and we all know there are many ups and downs along the way, but when you pursue your true calling, you have to know that on the other side of your challenges are your biggest opportunities yet! God makes you uncomfortable because that is the place we grow the most. Now, at the same time, he has given us the free will to decide not to overcome challenges as well. He has also allowed us the ability to control our thoughts and the ability to hear what others say as we endure those challenges, which is why when you are on a major mission, you MUST surround yourself by people that will not allow you to give up in spite of what you are hearing and seeing around you. People that can help you remain focused on the opportunities and be there to support and encourage you along the way, which is why I began this movement back in March of 2015 – www.co-opmovement.com. To provide an environment that will stir you up & challenge you to find your purpose and then provide the tools, resources and support for Entrepreneurs like you to go for it! So, your purpose is the number one key to success in business and in life. For this reason and this reason alone – IT

WILL NOT LET YOU GIVE UP! The journey of entrepreneurship is a long and winding road. There will be times where others would definitely throw in the towel, but with a purpose, you will find a way to persevere & be the inspiration for the others you are so desperately trying to help do the same through your business! You cannot quit because others are counting on you. If you read any of the top success stories out there, you will always hear that they were driven to find a way for reasons other than themselves. They always had a deep conviction to achieve and serve others. Otherwise, if it's solely about us, we could quit almost instantly and it would not impact or affect anyone else. So if you want my secret nugget to success – immediately make your business about others. Then find a way to commit and make it real as quickly as you can – this will act as your accountability to keep on truckin' when times get tough!

So how do you find your purpose? Well, I think that is the easiest thing in the world for OTHERS to identify, but in my experience, it's tough for people to see on their own. There are people that do see their true purpose, but are afraid of actually making the move too. But for the most part, what I've found over the years, is that people have trouble seeing what they were truly meant to be. This is partly because, for most, it is far different than what they are currently doing. Unfortunately, most of us pursue vocations based upon the amount of money they can make, not those which you are passionate about, but may not lead to a "comfortable living" or lifestyle. That's why I love to do this with Entrepreneurs, because they have already made the decision to pursue their dreams. They are usually stuck or struggling because they are not following their purpose – they are chasing money!

Fortunately for you, I can usually help you spot your purpose in less than 15 minutes after asking a few key questions. Isn't that exciting? So let's try and ask those questions now & hopefully by the time we are finished here, you will have an idea of your true purpose. If you find it, please visit the Co-Op Movement Facebook page and proclaim it to the world – this is the most exciting thing in the world to me and I love experiencing the joy, in the moment with people that have recently found their purpose, because it brings them to life! Wouldn't you want to add a sense of purpose and meaning to your life? It lies within your purpose! Otherwise, the alternative is waking up and pressing repeat each and every day, which quite frankly is the reason why most of you left your job to begin with, right?

You can easily spot an Entrepreneur lacking purpose because they are irritable, appear drained, negative, unmotivated and complaining about all of the customer work they have to do! That to me is a key indicator that there is no end in sight for them. The work they are enduring now, will only be replaced by more work, without purpose. There is no end – in their mind. However, when you find your purpose, you become instantly inspired and massively focused! Suddenly you want to grow your business and hire others, because you now have a vision as to why you need to expand and reach the people in the world that need you. Your business growth suddenly has purpose. Only you can decide where you currently stand. Only you can decide to try something differently! If you want to again find the independence, meaning, purpose, opportunity you once saw in your business with a purpose, then it's time to open your mind! Let's bring that fire and spark back!

Ok – so here are the questions I ask people to unveil their purpose. Take your time when answering these questions, after all, this is determining your future!

1. How do you spend your FREE time?
2. Who are you most excited to help and why?
3. By helping those people, what impact would you have on their lives and those around them?
4. Why MUST these people get help from you?
5. What fires you up about what's happening in the world today & if you could fix it, what would you do?

Usually, it doesn't take asking all 5 of these questions to determine the gifts that are present in the people I meet with, because their passion just reveals itself immediately. If you are like most, when you finally ask for help, you are willing to be vulnerable to others, which is why it only takes 15 minutes for someone like me to bring you back to life with purpose. What I recommend doing is talk through these questions with someone that will not judge and will constructively brainstorm with you. If you cannot find someone to help and you just can't figure it out, then contact my office at (866) 217-8425 and we would be happy to help.

In the meantime, let me give you a few examples of what I mean by finding your purpose. A few months back, I met with a person that just became a sponsor of the co-op movement, which is driven to help companies all over the United States find their mission and lead with it to grow their business with purpose. I could tell this person was drained and was looking to add purpose and meaning to her carpet cleaning business. So I asked how she spends her time each day and I found out that she was also a social worker that cares for children with disabilities. She was extremely passionate about it, but it didn't necessarily tie into a carpet cleaning business, or so she thought. Business was challenging, she was struggling to grow and found it difficult to team up and align with others in her industry to attract more referral business. I thought to myself, a team of home service providers would be awesome to help children in need. So I asked, what if you could team up with others in the home services industry to help make homes livable for children with disabilities? She thought it was great and I could sense a change in her almost instantly.

When you add a purpose far greater than yourself to anything you do, it instantly changes your life because you become aligned with our true intent as humans here on earth – to serve others we care about!

Here's another example. A passion coach & I were speaking following an event, where I offered a FREE vision setting session for attending. She shared with me her confusion on what to focus on because she has opportunities to pursue given needs in the marketplace for services like she offers, but I immediately re-directed the conversation to the questions I listed above. Before I share more let me say this, when I hear people are confused about overall direction of a company, it is because they are making decisions solely on opportunities to capitalize on revenue/sales and profits, which you are probably thinking, duh! But I will say this, in a world where people are currently trying to be everything to everyone, the opportunity lies in being true to yourself. So, I began to ask questions to determine how she got into this business & in her case, if you were going to help someone else find their passion, how did you find yours? From there, I learned that she, herself was stuck in a job, working out of a cubicle in corporate and looking for meaning (like many people out there). She happened to stumble upon a program that she is now a consultant with, that helped her find her passion & changed her life. Now, she wants to help others that are in those same situations find their passions as well. So remember when I asked the original question about choosing direction in her business, well she never mentioned helping people in a corporate setting to find their purpose & their passions. You will usually find the most success in helping people through something that you have gotten through yourself, especially in a coaching/consulting business! Your process becomes the gift you use to inspire the next person to find their way as well.

Do Not Chase the Market – Make the Market.

Your gifts can carve a brand new niche, as long as you are willing to recognize your true purpose and who you can help the most with the experiences and gifts you've been given! Now, she is driven to help the masses of corporate professionals break-free from their jobs and find a career or opportunity that supports their passions! That adds a whole lot of purpose to her business!

There are so many other examples to share on how and where to find your purpose, but the point is, you will find your purpose and opportunities to succeed most, hidden in the setbacks you've experienced in life. Most people unfortunately do not get this. Instead, they hide their mistakes and are embarrassed by them. However, I'm here to tell you that there isn't one perfect soul on this planet! Those experiences have given us ways to learn, improve, grow and share with others. If we learn through the process, that is truly an experience worth sharing & everyone has a way to help others get through the situations you have succeeded in overcoming! I don't care what business you are in, if you have a passion to help people like you, you can find a way to lead with that purpose! Success in life is learning that we are not perfect – believe it or not & that life is a journey of experiences that help us become the people that God intended us to be. So to find our purpose, we need to humbly look back on our experiences that very well started as a setback, that ended up fueling your life & asking who and how can I help others benefit from my experience? You don't have to be Oprah, Ellen or any other famous person to impact others. You just have to be willing to take the first step and that first step is to believe that if this made a difference in one life, it can make a difference in a thousand lives, a million lives or whatever you think you can do, then begin sharing it with everyone you come into contact with!

CHAPTER THREE

BECOMING A LEADER

....

"Lead with Your Mission and Your Business will Follow."
– Jeff Levin

How exciting, you now have a purpose that is bigger than yourself & your business. When you put things into perspective, you probably realize right away that you have a real ability to impact many lives, once you begin sharing it with others. Before beginning to get others involved though, it is important to put your mission in writing, so let's do that right, here, right now with a brand new, purpose driven mission statement.

Your mission statement should be S.M.A.R.T, which stands for Specific, Measurable, Achievable, Results Oriented & achieved within a Timeframe.

So let's fill in the blanks. My mission is to help/provide/create, etc. (enter number of people) in the (geographic region) (overcome or fix a problem) by (enter a timeframe).

After you write this down, then go to the Co-Op Movement Facebook Page with the hashtag #mission28m and post your mission tp become 1 of the 28 million companies impacted by the movement that is helping to re-define success across the United States. Please be sure to share it with your friends and followers as well and what you find is people will immediately latch onto your story and mission and want to share it.

By writing this down you've taken the first action step toward becoming a leader that will not only transform your business but impact communities in your area.

Now that you have a mission and it's written down, it's time to start communicating and sharing it everywhere you go, with every person you speak with. So how comfortable are you with what I call leading with your mission? Your job is not to be comfortable in business, it is to create impact. If you've never massively succeeded before, it takes doing things that make you massively uncomfortable first, in order to begin to move your own mission or movement. However, I will say, it is far from natural to lead with your mission, so let me share why it is important and how to ease the pain of venturing into the valley of the unknown.

I get that sharing your mission has nothing to do with your business and to me that is excellent, because when you first meet someone, they really don't care what you or what your business is about, they are more interested in you. So if you truly discover your mission and purpose, you will speak of it with a certain glow that will tell the people right away that you are about something more than the transaction. We once had a bookkeeper join our movement. As a Platinum Sponsor, they get one-to-one interaction and assistance from me, which is a great perk I must say for sponsoring at the highest level of the movement. So we were talking one day and she was explaining her business, but it was missing the fire and energy that was needed to really grow a company. So I asked her what she liked to do and she began to share her passion for gardening and growing organic food. She mentioned how toxic our soil is here in America compared to her native country and that she would love to help people understand this and help them grow true organic crops for their families. I asked her, well what if you made your mission about inspiring companies to not only grow through your services but also helping to grow organic plants the right way by asking everyone to dedicate a small plot of land in their backyards? How many plants would you need to feed the people in the area that need these crops most? She began to see that the purpose for her profits was to create sustainable growth for companies and in the community through raising organic crops to feed the hungry. She completely changed her company name and mission and began communicating her company in a different way. It's not an easy process to step out and be about something more in your community but I will say it again, as a business owner, you are in fact a community leader, and those who realize this will succeed.

Part of becoming a leader is your ability and courage to be able to stand out in front for what you believe in, even if it means you are the only one standing there. You have to believe that you will achieve your mission regardless if one more company chooses to come by your side to help you. That is someone that had complete conviction around what they do. What are you willing to stand out in front to achieve? A great mentor of mine, always says "Which hard do you want?" It's hard to stand out in front! It's hard to do things differently! It's hard to be broke and struggle doing it like everyone else.

Every large company was inspired by a mission to solve a big problem. So if you knew that to be true, then what would stop you from doing it? What would stop you from pulling an all nighter each and every night for the next two weeks to re-vamp your company and turn it into something that will not only inspire you to spend every waking hour working on it and in it, but also others to want to help you accomplish it? If you want to be massively successful, you have to do something that will reach and inspire the masses. Do you see yourself being the leader of that mission? If you don't, it's time to begin working on yourself and that is exactly why we have creating the Co-Opvertising™ Network platform and I am writing this book and building programs, because you need to work hard on becoming a leader first. Take the time right now to identify 5 things you need to improve upon to become an influential leader and then begin working on them by reading books or hanging around people that you recognize with the qualities you are looking for in yourself as a leader. I highly encourage you that before you begin over-analyzing yourself and what you need to "fix" first before you begin just getting out there and talking to people, is to simply reach out to someone you know or want to know and share it with them over coffee or tea.

Making connections at the mission level in business will guarantee long term connections in business, that will allow you to leverage in so many different ways to help you grow both your mission and your company. Leading with your mission shows people you are meeting and aligning with that you are about more than just the transaction, which will naturally accelerate the trust building process and get you to active business relationship faster which we will talk about later in the book.

The chapters to follow will focus on the strategy that I invented years ago based upon years of research and experience growing companies in the small business arena. It's called Co-Opvertising™! This single strategy will teach you the easiest way to capitalize and leverage the relationships you are building, all in an effort to build an active promotional and referral network. Most companies grow through networking, so why not get the most out of it? This strategy will bring purpose to the time you spend building relationships in business and help turn your network into a promotional army!

CHAPTER FOUR

GETTING THE MOST FROM YOUR NETWORKING

· ·

"Every trustworthy business owner is a credible endorsement inside their own sphere of influence." – Jeff Levin

Back in 2006, sitting on a lake in Indiana on a beautiful summer day, I came up with this concept called Co-Opvertising™ that I believed would revolutionize the growth of companies all across America. Mind you, this was before Facebook, texting or even smart phones! I had spent the previous 3 years building companies as a business coach and what I found after working with hundreds of companies was they rarely had a marketing budget, but they had no problem investing in networks and organizations, which meant their relationship capital was valuable. So the question I asked way back then was how can I create a concept that would allow companies that share a common interest & target market to gain exposure to each other's databases, friends and followers? The concept of Co-Opvertising™ was born!

It became my goal to make the hardest part of the customer acquisition & referral process, getting the foot in the door – the easiest part for myself and clients of mine. Are you ready to hear why I believe Co-Opvertising™ is the MOST effective form of advertising on the planet for small business owners and sales professionals? Here we go...

Do you ever wonder why the big brands like Nike, Adidas and others choose to hire celebrities to endorse their products? Because people admire and look up to them & want to use the same products they use in hope that they too can get similar results. There is the novelty, keeping up with the joneses theory as well, that supports the fact that well, people just want to have what others can't. In any event, endorsements work, because if Michael Jordan wears Hanes underwear, then I too want Hanes underwear.

So, let's apply this to the small business arena and why I believe that every credible, trustworthy business owner is a celebrity or credible endorsement inside their own sphere of influence. Small business owners do not have the marketing budgets to hire high-powered celebrity figures to endorse their products and services. In fact, they usually spend very little in marketing. What they do instead, is invest their time in networking to build relationships. They typically spend a significant amount of time with other business owners at networking functions, they invest time in each and every one of their clients before, during and after the sale because they know if they do a great job, their clients will tell their friends, family and followers. So, they may not have the hard capital to invest in high powered ads and endorsements, but what they do have is a significant amount of relationship capital built up in their client database. Their clients trust them. So if they were to recommend any products or services to the databases, their opinion would be trusted and well received – just like that of a celebrity, because a significant amount of trust and credibility has been built already. This holds true for every single successful small business owner out there.

So here's why this is such a powerful strategy. It takes years to build a quality database. I don't care if you are trying to build an email database or build up likes on Facebook or followers on Twitter, it takes time to build a quality database that is worthwhile and significant enough to market to. So, knowing everything I just shared above, why would anyone want to focus solely on building their own lists up, if they had the opportunity to use their network of strategic alliances to help promote their businesses? Imagine if you had 10 alliances with 1000 contacts in their database and each agreed to share your offer with them. That is prime exposure, referral quality exposure, in front of 10000 of the very people you would one day gain referrals from, when they are ready! That's huge. So my challenge to each of you, is why wait because you don't have to wait, all you have to do is be willing to offer value to these valuable alliances to give away to their databases! It's time to make the referral process predictable for once!

That is Co-Opvertising™ – building strategic and direct promotional opportunities by packaging your products or services as a gift for them to share as a gift to their valuable client databases.

And best of all, because you are giving away your offer as a gift, the leads all come to you. Imagine not having to chase people to buy your products or use your services? If you are a gift, people come to you because they want the gift. Attracting business becomes easy! Imagine if you had somebody promoting you regularly in every city, county or state to their clients? How would your business look? That's what's exciting about this, because it now adds purpose to your networking efforts. If you apply a laser sharp focus to find the exact people that would be perfect to partner up with in this way, your only challenge is finding the right number of strategic alliances that you need to meet your monthly and annual sales & profitability targets in your business! It's all math from there on out. Every company that has done this effectively has blown their business up & it's time to do the same for you. I'm a firm believer that if you nail your co-opvertisement, you will not need a single additional method of lead generation for your business- that is how effective this method of marketing can be if you do it correctly.

Valuing Your Co-Op Offers

Let me start off by saying that everyone buys their leads and their customers – even you! Do you believe that? This is called your customer acquisition cost. Your first step to fully understand the value that you are able to give, is to understand what you normally pay to acquire them anyway. Now you may say, that you have a 100% referral based business & that's great, but you most likely are a part of a network, chamber or niche association group that has membership fees and lunch fees that you attend & therein lies your costs in acquiring the customers you have, if you use those networks to drive referrals in your business.

To calculate your **acquisition cost**, follow this simple equation:

Total marketing, advertising, networks/association fees, meals/lunches

---

Total number of clients you have

Once you have an understanding of your acquisition costs, it is also very important to understand the **lifetime value** of your customers. What is lifetime value? Simply put, it's the total sales acquired from a customer over the lifespan that they actively purchase from you. This is very important because it is the return on investment per client – it's why you "buy" customers. To understand the lifetime value of your customers, you will need to review your financial system. Most financial systems like QuickBooks for example, have a standard report you can run by customer, that will give you the sum total by customer of all of the revenue received from that client. So, what I recommend doing is taking all the revenue generated & dividing it by the total number of clients you have had and that will tell you what the life time value of a customer is. Now, if you do not have a financial system in place & cannot determine your expenses easily, then I highly recommend that you consider my LevelUp Business Survival Training. Go to LevelUpMyBiz.com for more!

Targeting Your Offer

Now for those of you who were able to determine your costs, we are ready to take the next step to determine how to find something of value to share. I'm a firm believer that you will get whatever you aim for in life or in business. Many people try to generalize with their product or service offerings and fail to capture even their local market, because they are trying to appeal to the masses. While the ones that do well, target their market & focus their efforts. You may not capture everything with a targeted approach, but you will capture most of what you are aiming for & actually develop a niche for that offering.

But when we speak about Co-Opvertising™, it is not only important to understand the people that need your products or services, but also the other businesses that service these same companies, because those are the people that our referrals come from. These are what I refer to as strategic referral alliances or strategic alliances for short. Again, they are the companies that you either know or need to know that service the same target market as you – usually non-competing companies. So go through your contact list and make a list of all of the potential alliances you potentially have already.

When it comes to targeting potential alliances, it is important to think far outside of the traditional realm of targeting, because that's where all of the opportunity resides. You know your target audience just as well as your alliances, if not better, but it's important to know how you can add value to the customer experience that these individual businesses are constantly trying to create to WOW them. Most of the time, this will be a new approach and that's why it's important to brainstorm ideas alone first to determine ways to add value to their experience prior to meeting with them.

Determining the Number of Active Strategic Alliances Needed

Let's circle back to why building active strategic alliances are so important before we get into quantifying how many you need.

Remember, your alliances feed you referral business. In the case of Co-Opvertising™, your alliance are your promotional engine. They will provide you with the opportunity to build predictability into the referral process and it is our goal to show you how to 50X (increase by 50 times) your marketing power through Co-Opvertising™ like we have done for ourselves and so many others for 14 plus years. Now there is a difference between a strategic alliance and an active strategic alliance. An active strategic alliance is someone that is actively promoting your business to their list or customers as a gift to be redeemed through you. Your gift will make your alliances look great and it will open the doors of opportunity to the people they are referring anyway, so all this does is expedite the referral process and make it more predictable. If you had 10, 20, or event 50 alliances actively sharing your business as a gift to their clients, your business would be moving like a well-oiled machine wouldn't it?

In order to determine the number of alliances you need on your promotional team or as we like to call it, your GrowthPOD, you need to know and understand two things:

1. Your sales goals
2. Your average conversion rate

Determining your sales goals may seem simple, but it's important that you understand what your sales need to be in order to achieve break-even profitability in your business. If you are unsure how to determine what your sales goals should be, please visit www.levelupmybiz.com and request a FREE consultation with a LevelUp Coach or sign up for my e-coaching program that will help you determine your numbers as well as the core sales and marketing strategies that will launch your company into growth mode!

Your conversion rate can be determined by having a solid understanding of your incoming leads and where they are coming from. You don't need anything fancy really, except a simple tracking sheet designed to help you track the leads coming in. After setting up your lead tracking sheet, (which I give you the one I've used to build $1 million dollar franchiseable businesses, just go to www.levelupmybiz.com) all you need to do determine your closing rate, is to divide the total customers closed by your total number of leads for a given period.

Having a solid understanding of your break-even sales goals, leads required and conversion rate will help you to determine just how many active strategic alliances you will need.

Marketing 10 x 10

For now, however, let's assume that you are not tracking your leads, so it is important to set a goal to establish a minimum of 10 strategic alliances. The more marketing strategies you have in place, the better. To illustrate this point, consider this: Imagine a person standing on the edge of a diving board. There is only 1 support at the far left of the platform, which making the board unstable and flimsy. There is only 1 support, so if that fails – the diver will fall into the pool. However, what would happen if there were ten supports that were spaced evenly across the length of the diving board? The board with support is now, stable and strong. Well the same holds true for your business. Marketing is sporadic at times, so it's important to have multiple strategies in place at any given time to ensure that if one fails, you have 9 others to fall back on! So, your initial goal should be to ensure that at any given time, you have 10 active strategic alliances that are actively sharing your Co-Opvertising™ Offer as a gift with their clients. Until you have a firm understanding of your leads & conversion rate, continue to build alliances!

CHAPTER FIVE

CREATING VALUABLE CO-OPVERTISING™ OFFERS

....

"Being a gift for others to share is the best way to open the doors of opportunity!" – Jeff Levin

Now that you understand who to target and what we pay for our clients traditionally, it's time to craft a Co-Opvertising™ offer or opportunity to present to the different strategic alliances we already have and prospective alliances we meet in the future.

The goal of this exercise is to create an opportunity/offer that is so good, they just cannot pass it up! We want them to say YES, let's make this happen right now. So as you are brainstorming, it is important that your offers or opportunity have each of the following elements built within:

1. The offer has to be valuable
2. There should be a strong need/or desire to have what you are offering
3. The offer should provide a WOW factor for your alliances process

4.   The offer should be positioned as a gift from your alliance
5.   The offer should be given with no strings attached
6.   There should be an expiration to redeem the gift

The value of your offer, must be real tangible value the end user needs. As the owner, you have to place your ego aside and put yourself in the shoes of the end user and ask, would they value the offer on the table. This should not be a FREE consultation or something of unrealistic value. It needs to be something that your target audience values and would purchase what you are offering, if they were not getting it FREE.

This is where the challenge lies for most in determining what to offer. The goal is to offer the highest, real value, at the lowest hard costs possible. We calculated earlier what you typically "invest" to purchase or acquire new clients, so you have the ability to go as high as that in hard costs, but our goal is to minimize expenses as much as possible.

The best Co-Opvertising™ Offers are those that have high perceived value with minimal hard costs. Offers are different dependent upon each business, but in the end, they accomplish the same goals always – your offer enables you to build strategic alliances and they also give you an opportunity to leverage your value to gain exposure in front of other people's databases – two very important factors that will contribute to accelerating the growth of your business.

The best way to illustrate Co-Opvertising™ ideas are through examples. You can find an entire list of examples in the back of the book, but for the purposes of discussion, let's focus on a few key examples. If you would like assistance in helping you determine your offer, you can sign-up as a sponsor of the Co-Op Movement & receive a meeting with a Co-Opvertising™ Expert.

Co-Opvertising™ Example No. 1 – The Shower Cake

Business Type: Wedding Cake Stylist

Target Market: Brides

This is the story of the shower cake example that has become quite infamous in the Co-Opvertising™ Network after sharing it so many times from stage at our live events and workshops. It is now everyone's goal to find their "shower cake" for their particular business.

Years ago, my wife Lisa decided to become a cake stylist & began making beautiful wedding cakes. They were the fancy cakes that you now see on TV, that are worth thousands of dollars. We didn't have a whole lot of money to invest in advertising & marketing and at the time, social media did not exist, so we had to find creative ways to get the word out. So we came up with a great offer, something that we could give away of value that had low hard costs, but high perceived value to the end user. We landed on giving away a FREE shower cake which had a value of $200 – that's a pretty good value!

After deciding upon the offer, we began searching for the best service providers in the wedding industry that would like to give their clients this fabulous offer when they became their clients. What we found worked best were photographers and florists. So we printed off stacks of post card sized marketing pieces and gave them to the photographers & florists to hand their clients upon closing. They were excited to give these away because it added a tremendous value to their services, plus it absolutely blew their clients away, so they couldn't wait to give away the next one! Now this offer was treated just like a promotion, meaning, the offer had to be redeemed within a short period of time. As a result, we consistently received leads wanting the FREE shower cake! Now, here's the really exciting part -99% of the leads that contacted us through this method turned into paying customers for the wedding cakes as well! This is the true power of Co-Opvertising™! Because we didn't just give away the shower cake when they called. We walked them through our normal customer acquisition process that led to the sale of the wedding cakes worth over $1200 each. So, in this example, we gave away $200 in value that had close to 2 hours of time & $30 in hard costs to make the shower cake that 99% of the time, landed a wedding cake sale! Not a bad conversion rate after spending no money on advertising. All we did was understood the motivation of our strategic alliances (photographers & florists) and created a co-op offer that would WOW their customers and also fulfill their customer's needs. It's important to note, though, that there were no strings attached to this offer and we were fully prepared to make the shower cakes for free, but never had to because there were other needs to fulfill. Since we led with giving and our products were awesome, they naturally went with us for their wedding cakes! Which affirms what I've always believed. When it comes to outsourcing services for anything, people want to deal with those they know, like and trust! What better way to build trust than through a gift and endorsement? An endorsement from someone else, transfers the trust that has been built through the individual who shared you & the gift – well, who really ever turns down an awesome gift from a friend? This is why I truly believe Co-Opvertising™ needs to be a household name for everyone in business or in sales!

As I mentioned earlier, I use this example frequently to illustrate the power of Co-Opvertising™ in blog posts, speaking engagements and during coaching sessions because it is tangible and easy for people to understand. But, before moving on to another example, let's go through why this was so effective.

1. The offer was valuable – a $200 shower cake is valuable to any bride.
2. There was a strong need - Every bride has a wedding shower & we knew they also need to purchase a wedding cake, which was the driver behind choosing the shower cake as our offer.
3. The offer should provide the WOW factor and it surely did! Presenting it at the end of the sales process, made the brides feel extra special.
4. There was an expiration on the offer so it created a sense of urgency in the bride to contact us which helped to make the referral process more predictable.
5. When the brides called, we did not just take orders for the free shower cake. Instead, we put them through our normal customer acquisition process to attempt to land the wedding cake as well and we did – 99% of the time!
6. Finally, there were no strings attached on the offer – we were prepared to deliver on the offer of a FREE Shower Cake, regardless if they purchased the wedding cake. Incidentally, only one person did not end up purchasing the wedding cake through us & although they could have still taken advantage of the offer, they declined.

Here's another example to illustrate the thought process I go through each time to brainstorm creative opportunities for potential alliances & Co-Opvertising™ offers.

Co-Opvertising™ Example No. 2 – The Fashion Show

Business Type: Fashion Consultant

Target Market: Women

A direct sales professional came on my show, Co-Opie Talk (Follow us on Facebook @coopietalk to watch our show every morning at 9am central) one day to promote their investment in a new clothing line for women. She had been stumped for quite some time on how she can structure a Co-Opvertising™ offer for her company, so I began to ask her questions. The two questions I asked to kick off the brainstorming session are the same two questions I ask each and every time I meet with people:

1. **What businesses attract women (or people you are targeting) in high volumes?**
2. **How can we add value to their experience?**

Many types of companies attract women in high volume but we landed on salons and professional speakers that host large events for one main reason – they are accessible within her network and our network, where if you are not a part of, I would highly recommend joining – just go to www.co-opmovement.com or find us on Facebook by searching Co-Opvertising™ network and join a network in your area. I am all about keeping things simple and easily creating opportunities. So we thought it would be excellent as a door opener to build an alliance with the salon stylists and also the professional speakers to provide an outfit for them to wear from the clothing line at no cost. We then set out to arrange, market and pay for a private, VIP fashion show for their clients! (This idea can work for the entire salon or for individual stylists, whatever one comes first! It is my recommendation to approach the individual stylists and offer to host a fashion show for their clients alone first, but eventually it could lead to a fashion show for the entire salon and the clients of all the stylists) Imagine all of the clothing customers they can potentially get for bringing value like this to the salon? Best of all, this company could partner with other vendors to share in the expense as well. Which brings me to the third question I always ask:

3. Who else can I get involved to assist in covering the costs of the idea?

Now of course there will be costs associated with making this VIP night a success, but what you have done is arranged an super targeted opportunity to be in front of a business's clientele that has high traffic. So, now it's time to use this opportunity to build alliances with businesses that need that traffic as well, to enhance the experience of the event, plus they can help cover the costs. There are always others that will want to be involved. To seal the deal with your alliances, offer access to the leads that come to the event/show and you will easily find others that will want to participate! In this example, we were able to involve jewelry reps, caterers, invitation companies and others that could help! Have fun with the process and the excitement will show when you meet with your alliances for the first time!

How about one more example?

Co-Opvertising™ Example No. 3 – Inspirational Framed Photo

Business Type: Travel Agent

Target Market: Business Owners

Travel agents typically work on 100% commission and are paid independently, so it's difficult for them to get outside of their situation, most of the time, because they don't have a ton of wiggle room when it comes with their packages.

When we began our discussion, it was not necessarily intuitive that we go after business owners, because she was interested in capturing anyone that is planning on vacationing in the near term (like every other travel agent positions themselves). Obviously, Co-Opvertising™ takes people far outside the box, so we began the thought process with the following question:

Who attracts a large/consistent volume of people that will most likely desire to go on vacation?

She lucked out here, because I happened to be an ideal target for an alliance with this person, because as a success coach/master business builder, it is my goal to inspire companies to grow and develop to the point to where companies work so that the owners don't have to so much & they can go on vacation! Learn more at www.levelupmybiz.com. One thing I have personally done with my clients is after they express interest in using my services, our admins always ask our prospects if you met your goals and your business was where you ultimately want to be, what would you be doing? They would usually tell us, something like "Be on a Beach" or "Go Fishing" or whatever. So what I would do is I would find a picture of what their answer was & I slapped my quote "Choice... The Difference Between Wanting or Having!" on the picture, framed it & then personally delivered it to their office along with the information they needed to prepare for my appointment with them. I always tried to place the photo on their desk or somewhere they could see it & every time I came back for the appointment, that photo was right where I put it! It worked well for appointments that actually held and it really helped focus my clients because that in fact became a visual for their goal. So long explanation to – this is a very valuable strategy that a travel agent can approach and offer to do for people that do seminars or events consistently.

So the Question is, How Can I Add Value to the Coaches Client Experience?

By bringing this strategy and offering to provide this $7 framed photo, you now have an opportunity to get in front of people that will be going on vacation for just $7 & give you an insert into their folders for offers on trips to their destination of choice.

So, you may be thinking, this works out well for the coach or presenter, but how will the travel agent make money? Well what they can do is also ask to have the coach include this on their feedback forms so that the people in attendance at their events provide them with where they would like to go on vacation and when. The agent would get the list of attendees from the coach after their events & then they can develop a vacation accountability email campaign designed to keep their trips at the top of mind & as they approach their dates, they can contact them directly to push them over the edge. Business owners need to sometime be told to take vacations, so this is a great way to condition them to take more trips – even if they are short get aways. What a great opportunity for travel agents!

This is an example of adding value to a business, in order to get an opportunity to sell something of value to their clients.

If you are interested in more examples, please visit the back of the book where I share several more examples of ways companies are Co-Opvertising™.

If done correctly, Co-Opvertising™ opens the doors to acquiring strategic alliances and consistent referrals than ever before. All because you made a choice to find a way to help someone else first!

CHAPTER SIX

EXECUTING CO-OPVERTISING™ OPPORTUNITIES

∙∙∙∙∙∙∙∙∙∙∙∙∙∙∙∙∙∙∙∙∙∙∙∙∙∙∙∙∙∙∙∙∙∙∙∙∙∙

"Give what you are seeking" – Jeff Levin

The way to implement your Co-Opvertising™ opportunities will depend upon the way your strategic alliances interact with their clients and how they plan to introduce the offer. So, before you share how you can help them, let me introduce you to the different ways you can deliver an effective Co-Op Marketing Campaign.

Direct Mail Co-Opvertising™

Direct Mail is extremely effective but it is the most costly strategy. Now in any case, when you volunteer to cover all expenses and do all the work, it increases the likelihood of them following through with the strategy. If you decide direct mail is how you wish to execute the campaign, you will need to arrive at the meeting with a sample campaign for them to see, review and approve. The most common way to do this is to craft a thank you letter of sorts on your alliances letterhead, addressed from them that expresses their appreciation for their client & introduces your company offer, event or opportunity as a free and valuable gift for being excellent clients. The only thing your alliance should have to do is to put together the mailing list and provide you with their letterhead (or their logo so you can re-create it with their permission). Again, it is more costly, but is very effective, considering many people do not use snail mail anymore & under these circumstances they will be receiving a message that is similar to a thank you card!

Custom Greeting Card Co-Opvertising™

www.cardsanywhere.com, a distributor of Send Out Cards, allows you to print on-demand or in bulk custom cards from their site. With this option, you can become a distributor and earn some money, while getting your alliances setup as distributors as well. Then, all you need to do is craft a message promoting your new alliance to your list in your account and then when they are ready to return the favor, they will need to create an account, import their list & send your message out to their account. I highly recommend if you are going this route, that you do 100% of the work for your alliance to ensure the campaign is executed on-time!

Email Co-Opvertising™

The easiest and most effective way to Co-Opvertise via email is using a system that I developed called GrowthPOD.com. This online system allows you to easily add content from others in your co-op marketing campaigns to share with your clients. GrowthPOD works on a credit system. You only pay when you choose to self-promote & you earn credits when you share Co-Opvertisements from others. So, to share content from your new potential alliances with your email list, all they need to do is create a FREE account and connect with you in the GrowthPOD system which is very similar to connecting on Facebook. Once your connection is accepted, then you will be able to grab any Co-Opvertising™ offer from the people you are connected with and add them to your campaign. You can add and promote several of your alliances in your campaigns, which I encourage everyone to do on a monthly basis. It really takes the work out of creating and managing your e-newsletters and is a great way to provide new and fresh content to your clients to keep them interested in between purchases! Go to GrowthPOD.com to learn more! Sponsors of the Co-Opvertising™ Movement are able to use GrowthPOD FREE (we give you credits based upon your sponsorship level – top sponsors get unlimited credits). To become a sponsor visit Co-Opvertising™network.com/sponsorship now!

If you plan to utilize GrowthPOD.com to execute your strategies, we again recommend taking all of the work away from your strategic alliances to create their accounts, add their content and lists to the GrowthPOD.com system, that way you can nearly guarantee your message goes out when you need it to. Because remember, the campaigns need to be delivered from your alliances to be effective. The benefit of using a system like GrowthPOD.com is once you are setup and in the system, future campaigns will be easy. So, although there are costs associated with it, I would pay for their account setup by contacting GrowthPOD.com at 866.217.8425 or invest the time to do it yourself, because there is tremendous value in your strategic alliances databases that will save you years in building a list on your own.

The most effective method of using the system is to utilize the same approach as we recommended in the direct mail approach in GrowthPOD as well. Create a campaign on your alliances branded template that is designed to thank their customers for being excellent and for being so awesome, you have arranged an opportunity to experience your business. The entire campaign should be about your company offering, but it's sent from your alliances account. If you need assistance in writing your messages, please contact us at 866.217.8425. We are expert sales copy writers and would be happy to assist you in setting up your clients and messaging in the system for optimal results.

Using this methodology, wouldn't it be great if you had an alliance message going out from your alliances daily that promoted your business? Exactly! This is why we are so excited for everyone learning this very important strategy to grow their business.

We have found over the years that the best way to get people in the habit of cross promotion is to offer it as an opportunity for others first. They always say that if you want anything in life, give it to someone first! So, if you want someone to promote you via email to their lists, then offer to do that first and of course, we recommend using GrowthPOD.com because it will position them for ongoing opportunities for cross promotion, since all of the information is there already!

On your end, it is recommended that you setup a regular, on-going monthly e-news publication in GrowthPOD.com and invite the people that you wish to be in front of to be featured in your next publication going out at the end of the month. Most will never turn down the opportunity to be promoted free, so they will say yes & when they do, provide them the instructions to create an account on GrowthPOD.com, add their content and list to the system & then after it's setup and sent, ask them if they wouldn't mind sending out something to their database as well and help them get through the process of setting up their campaign in the system. Yes, you will have to become versed in GrowthPOD and you will take on a support role to make that happen, but again, what is it worth to get in front of your future referrals? In my experience, it was the difference of me having to promote and fill my events, versus doing it through the leverage I possessed in my network. The only stipulation is you have to be willing to help your alliances through the process so that their campaign goes out at the right time to meet your company's goals. You can always outsource that activity as well to the GrowthPOD.com support for a nominal fee. Call today at 866.217.8425 to learn more about this service.

Social Media Co-Opvertising™

Social Media is easy to share others, but doesn't get as much traction as email or direct mail, but nevertheless, let's talk about how to get the most out of Co-Opvertising™ on social media. If you are reading this, chances are you are a part of an online Co-Opvertising™ Network group on Facebook. If you aren't, take the time right now to search now and get involved with people that are doing business this way.

So, if you are friends with people within the network, then simply watch their news feeds and when you see something worth promoting, share it with your friends and encourage them to utilize their services if it makes sense for your audience and aligns with your values and make sure you tag the person as well, so they know who it came from. After doing this and they thank you for it (which they will), use this as an opportunity to dive in and learn more about how you can help them and present something that you wish for them to share as well. The more people promoting and sharing your business, the better! And since you are a part of an online network with a culture driven around helping others first, it is best to begin with targeting alliances in our network.

Now that you understand 3 of the main ways to deliver your Co-Opvertising™ campaign, let's discuss how do you know which avenue to pursue. Based upon experience, it is recommended that you choose the way easiest for them to execute and that is via social media. That way they don't have to pull a mailing list or email list together. So it is recommended that you begin through social media, then after getting to know them better, find an opportunity to engage via email as well. Unless you are doing something that requires them to touch it, feel it or taste it, I would stay away from snail mail due to the expense & logistics.

CHAPTER SEVEN

50X YOUR PROMO POWER

. . . .

"Every alliance you build exponentially increases your promotional power!" – Jeff Levin

Now that we have a Co-Opvertising™ strategy and offer, it's time to get to work building our team of strategic alliances or as we like to call it, building your GrowthPOD. Your GrowthPOD is your team of active promotional alliances that will help you in in getting 50 times the amount of promotional power you could ever get on your own. Every active alliance you build, exponentially increases your reach. Think about how large your client list or prospecting database is? In our experience, the average entrepreneur has a list or audience 500-1000 people. So, if you build a GrowthPOD of 10 or more active alliances, you will literally 10X your promotional power! But why stop there? As much as you probably network online or offline, you could very easily 50X your business. How many alliances will it take to 50X your Business?

Accelerating the Referral Process

Before we go any further, let's breakdown how the referral process typically works, just to illustrate the power of this strategy. Think about the alliances you have right now that have referred you business in the past. Do you remember the process you endured to build enough trust in them before they trusted your business enough to refer it? It probably required you to have coffee or lunch several times to get to know each other over a long period of time after seeing them several times at networking functions.

In my experience, it can take years to develop enough trust and rapport with you, before referrals begin to take place. And even then, the referrals rarely flow enough to be predictable. But yet, when you speak with most business owners they will tell you that they get all of their business or prefer to get their business from referral sources. So if your number one lead source was from referrals, wouldn't you want that process to be predictable?

So what's the key ingredient to accelerating the referral process? You guessed it – TRUST! What I am about to share with you will change the way you approach any relationship you have in your life, but most importantly will put your business relationship building on the fast track path to active referrals.

The key to build trust with anyone is to approach people with the genuine interest in helping them without the expectation of anything in return! That's it!

The most effective way of doing this is to ask questions to learn as much about them as possible & listen for ways that you can help them first. If you are seeking strategic alliances that you want to share your co-op offer, then the best way to get them to do it is to help them put one together for themselves. This will enable you or someone you know to share their business and help them first! This allows you to be a gift right from the start & it's the best kind of gift, because the knowledge never goes away. Plus it helps them grow their business, which everyone will appreciate.

The point to remember on why trust will occur so much faster than normal, is that you gave them what you are looking to get from them eventually first and regardless of whether or not you get the opportunity right then doesn't matter, because you have instantly broken the trust barrier, because you genuinely wanted to help them first! We encourage you to be a gift first, so that others will want to one day reciprocate the favor to you as well.

Once we get to trust in a relationship and we are willing to help others achieve their goals, they will be ecstatic to help you achieve yours as well & that's where your co-op offer will come into play.

Building Trusted Alliances

The best place to build alliances in my very biased opinion is of course The Co-Opvertising™ Network, but you can most definitely do this in any environment that attracts entrepreneurs. However, in the Co-Op, members have the ability to benefit from working in a culture and environment structured to allow you to succeed in an optimal way using the strategies and concepts we've been speaking about throughout this book!

CHAPTER EIGHT

BUILDING ACTIVE STRATEGIC ALLIANCES IN THE CO-OPVERTISING™ NETWORK

....

"When you join a network, your job is to become as attractive as a lighthouse, so people gravitate to you!" – Jeff Levin

The internet and social media has disrupted traditional business networking. You now can connect with and qualify people that you wish to dive deep into beneficial relationships faster than ever. No longer is it necessary to sit in a room with people you can't work with to find the 1-2 people you can.

The Co-Opvertising™ Network has both an online and offline component that allows you to maximize your time and find opportunities faster than any other environment and it is our goal to provide a long term environment for entrepreneurs to grow and succeed. **Take the time now to join our public online**

network on Facebook by searching for the Co-Opvertising™ Network and ask to join. When you do, you have access to several thousand people combined that are trained and on a mission to grow by helping others first.

Becoming a "Lighthouse" in the Co-Opvertising™ Network

In networking, you have the option of being as attractive as a lighthouse or like that person running around shining their flashlight in everyone's eyes saying, "Hey! Look at me!". What sounds like a better idea? I hope you agreed, that being a lighthouse is the best option. A lighthouse stands in one place and attracts others to them using their light source, which can be seen from miles away. When you join or partake in a network, whether it be online or offline, you become an attractive source or a lighthouse, when you are in complete alignment with the culture of the organization and you become the answer to what most people need. In short, you become a hub within the network or as some call it, a "connector". Your goal should be to become a hub of the network.

As we mentioned earlier, the key to building trust quickly is by helping others first, which is why we have created an environment like the Co-Opvertising™ Network, because we know that you have to get to trust, before you can get down to business, so why not focus entirely on building trusting relationships. The Co-Opvertising™ Network is not a place for self-promotion, in fact it is not permitted. Instead, we encourage our members to utilize the online group to promote others, build relationships, ask questions and inspire others to grow and succeed. When you choose to participate in this environment, you should use it to build your sales and promotional team, not your client base.

So, I know what you are thinking – if I can't promote my business there then what should I do? The answer is simple. Utilize the group to open the doors to new strategic relationships and nurture the ones you already have! When you do, you open the opportunity to not just serve the individual, but all of their clients. This makes the time that you invest in building relationships with individuals most worthwhile, considering you spend quite a bit of time with the people you are trying to develop into referral partners.

Can this be a helpful approach to other organizations and online groups or forums too? Yes it is and we highly encourage you to apply these same practices when you network in other environments as well, but if you want to be setup for complete success, join and participate in a Co-Op Network nearest you.

Getting Started in the Online Co-Opvertising™ Network

When you join any network, organization or company, your goal should be to become a go-to resource within the environment you are operating. Within the Co-Opvertising™ Network or any other network for that matter, there are a vast number of industries participating which can make it a bit overwhelming to simply jump in. By now you should have an excellent way to work together with most people you meet (your co-op offer or co-opvertisement), so instead of focusing on the masses in the network, we recommend making it a goal to target the business categories that would make excellent strategic alliances for your business. This will focus your efforts and make it far more manageable to navigate the large pool of companies in the group.

Engaging in the Co-Opvertising™ Network Online

Your goal should be to utilize the online network as an opportunity to open doors of opportunity to new relationships with potential alliances in the network. So, once you have your Co-Opvertising™ Offer in place and understand the business categories to target, you should begin posting and contacting members of the group in an effort to help them first by presenting them with opportunities. Here's an example of a message you can post publicly or private message to the people in your participating Co-Op Network.

Hi my name is [Name]. I am with [tag your business Facebook page]. We do [this, this and this…] I am looking for [list the types of businesses you'd like to meet] in [areas] that would be interested in offering [describe your offer] to your clients or being a part of this. If you are interested in learning more, please comment below.

I always say that you should be meeting with 2-3 new potential alliances each week, but the more people you meet with, the more opportunities you have to become a lighthouse or hub in your network quickly, but by all means – work at your own pace. I do however have a rule of thumb that applies to every business I've ever worked with. You should be spending 80% of your time doing sales and marketing activity in your company. Until you have enough sales opportunities, you should be fully booked with alliance appointments. So if you have the time, fill it with strategic alliance appointments, with a goal to build a promotional army of alliances that will work to promote your business to fill your calendar with sales appointments and customers.

Now, in large organizations like the Co-Op Network, there will be many opportunities to meet with and help people. It is important that you properly qualify and categorize the people that want to meet with you into a few simple categories that allow you to allocate time appropriately. For your initial alliance meetings, I recommend meeting online first using a video conferencing platform like zoom.us, Facebook or Facetime to allow you to meet and get to know the people that have responded in an efficient manner. These meetings should be 20-30 minutes max with a purpose of learning about the person, their mission and how you can help them. If it's decided that the relationship makes sense to delve in deeper, then setup a longer online or offline meeting. If you have an alliance that is talking about a way to immediately benefit, then obviously allocate time accordingly.

Engaging in the Co-Opvertising™ Network Offline

The Co-Opvertising™ Network is a movement and therefore, we host live events throughout the country where you can build a massive amount of connections, gain a massive amount of inspiration and education that will enable you to grow your business and we do it all by helping others first. As a new business or someone new to the Co-Op, we recommend that you quickly attend a Co-Op Movement Live Event to get you engaged right away. As a sponsor of the Co-Op Movement, you have the ability to attend our events FREE anywhere in the country (while seats remain). So mark your calendars and ensure you become a sponsor and attend all of our live events and you will have more opportunities than ever before! To become a sponsor or upgrade, go to www.Co-Opvertisingnetwork.com/sponsorship today.

Our events are unique in that we strategically connect you with people that you need to meet with a goal of 50xing your promotional opportunities in business. How would your business look with 50 active alliances promoting your business? As a sponsor you can attend events anywhere across the US as long as you can get there!

When you attend a Co-Op Movement Live Event, we encourage you to come prepared with a way that others can work with you & a genuine interest of getting to know the people we strategically place you in contact with during the event. If you do, it is impossible to not meet 30-40 new people in one day!

I Attended an Event, Now What?

You are excited and inspired after attending a Co-Op Movement Live Event! Floating on cloud nine, ready to tackle the world having just met 40 new people that can help you grow your company! Now what?

Well, you've probably heard this before but the fortune lies truly in your ability to follow-up, or in some cases follow through on the conversations held at the event.

So this is why at our events, I would recommend to actively listen and be a business card taker at the event. I learned long ago that if you took business cards, you could control the next steps in the relationship and this can easily be done by telling your alliance that you are fresh out of cards, but can surely take yours and follow up to schedule a time to talk or meet? Would that be ok with you? Of course it would be right? So, now they are expecting you to follow-up and I recommend to immediately begin that process later in the day or the next day. For example, you could immediately send a thank you message to all the contacts you met and remind them that you would be calling soon to schedule a time, but if they can take a look at their calendars and let you know the best day to meet next week, that would be excellent!

Meeting with New Strategic Alliances

Congratulations! You have landed appointments to meet with people that have an interest learning about ways you can work together. Before we get into a general format on what to cover in your first encounter, it's important to understand how relationships are formed:

The foundation in any relationship is trust. What I'm about to share with you will build trust in people faster than ever before, ultimately leading to productive, active business relationships that work to make referrals more predictable! So here's the secret...

This Meeting should be 100% focused on THEM.

When you focus on others with genuine interests to help, they will quickly realize you care. When people know that you care, they care what you know and have to say. Genuinely helping others first is always the way to go, to accelerate your own growth!

So ponder this one for a second...

If you want to gain exposure in front of their clients by them choosing to share your offer, then why don't you find a way to do this for them first? Be what you want in others & the chances of attracting the same is good! You can do this in a few different ways, both being equally effective.

Everyone always needs help marketing and growing their businesses, so when the time comes, ask them what kind of current offers and promotions they have going on right now. They will most likely not have very attractive offers that would work as well as a co-opvertisement would, so make the goal of the meeting to help them determine how to package their offering like a co-op offer that you can share with your clients. So while you are preparing for your meeting, brainstorm some of the best offers that your new potential strategic alliance could offer to your clients as a gift so you could share it. That way, when it comes time to brainstorm their offer, you look and sound like a marketing guru, when in fact, all you did was prepare for the meeting!

The goal would be for them to ask, how can I help you too and when they respond, you share your Co-Opvertising™ offer (that you've developed) that you would like for them to share with their clients. Now, don't get discouraged if they don't immediately reciprocate, in fact, go in not expecting anything from this because it could very well take a few meetings to get the opportunity, but remember, the best way to build trust is help people in a genuine, no strings attached fashion, so just trust that it will come back to you 10 fold and it will!

How to Help Your Alliances First

As mentioned in the previous paragraph, you have to go into your alliance meeting prepared with several ways to help them first. If you want their help in growing your business, which you should, then be prepared to help spread the word about their business first. Here are some of the ways you can help them.

Promote Your Alliances in your Monthly Co-Op e-Newsletter

This is very simple when using www.GrowthPOD.com which is FREE to use. Simply setup a monthly Co-Op e-Newsletter and then coach them on the type of offers or content you think your readers would appreciate most with them. If you become a sponsor of the Co-Op Movement at a higher level, you are assigned a Co-Op Agent that will actually setup, design and do the work to ensure you are actively promoting others in your e-newsletter, which of course opens the doors of opportunity for you to promote them as well.

Promote them on the Co-Opvertising™ Network Online Group

A very powerful way of helping the people you meet with is by sharing them with the group online. You may not realize this, but when you participate in the Co-Op Network our network becomes your network. Therefore, whether you can directly assist the people you sit down with or not, it is important to share them with the group, because someone else is bound to be able to help them too and worst case scenario, you will open the doors of opportunity for them to meet others. Be sure to post a selfie or what we like to call, a Co-Opie of the two of you meeting in the group and tag them in the post so they know you did it and chances are they will return the favor. What's best about this is that if you are consistently meeting with 2-3 new people every week and posting the photos and outcomes of the meeting, you will make it very attractive for others to want to meet with you. Yes, you become a lighthouse in the Co-Op and known as a person that is interested in helping others first.

Activating Your Alliances

The overall intent in investing the time and energy to build strategic alliances is to create active promotional partners for your business. But why? Well, to make the referral process predictable and repeatable of course! Why else do it? You cannot operate a business if you cannot predict the patterns and cycles of your company, so it's important to have as many active alliances promoting your Co-Opvertising™ Offer as possible. Let's hold the bar high and shoot for 50 active alliances, but within the initial 30-60 days, make it a goal to build 10. We call that 10Xing your promotional power through Co-Opvertising™. What would your business look like if you had 10 times the number of people promoting your business to their clients? How about 50? What about 100? It's time to network with intention and purpose. You should not be joining organizations to get clients from the members. Your job is to align with the members and make them your stronger sales agents. Focusing on selling to individuals creates transactional relationships. Building alliances allows you to create long term, leveraged relationships that create win-win opportunities to capitalize on wide-spread exposure.

So, when you go to convert your alliances into active strategic alliances, it's important to consider the following when crafting your opportunity:

1. Ensure that you control the materials or communications sent to their prospects promoting the opportunity. Yes, you will have to design the marketing piece, but it is well worth it, because you control the timeline to implementation.
2. Ensure that your offer has a deadline that meets your business needs. As a business owner, it is your obligation to understand the number of leads you need on a monthly basis to meet your goals. So for example, if you received 100 leads and converted 50 to new customers, then you will

have to have enough alliances sharing your offer to drive in 100 leads to meet your goals.

3. Ensure you test and measure the results of your campaign regularly and adjust. However, do not change an offer that is profitable and working. It may get boring, but business should be boring.

By focusing on the outcomes of your networking, it is possible to get so much more out of the time and energy you spend building relationships in business. Think for a moment about the number of people you have met with for coffee or lunch, that you have never received a referral from or a promotional opportunity from in the past. Now, imagine having the opportunity to meet with them again. How would you reposition the meetings to achieve your desired outcome of leaving with an active strategic alliance? Go back and reactivate your dormant relationships right now!

Closing Opportunities Through Co-Opvertising™

Your Co-Opvertising™ offer is an opportunity to get your prospects in the door. The quality of your sales process or funnel will determine how effective you are in closing sales opportunities from this point forward. If you do not have a sales process or funnel in place, you can become a sponsor of the Co-Op Movement now (www.Co-Opvertisingnetwork.com/sponsorship) and get my 52 Week LevelUp e-Coaching Program FREE that will walk you through the same sales process I've used to create million dollar companies or you can go to www.levelupmybiz.com to purchase the program. Generally speaking though, your Co-Op Offer is a door opener to get access to people. It's usually FREE, but leads them to a purchase and it is very important that you understand, that when you receive calls or emails to redeem your offer that you first, walk them through your normal customer acquisition process to determine if there is any other way you can assist them. If you are smart, you will structure your offer, so that they not only need your offer, but also need the upsell as well, similar to the shower cake, wedding cake upsell! Make sure that in the end, there is a strong, compelling reason to go with you on the upsell now, but if they do not choose to purchase anything that you ask them if they know anyone else that could benefit from your offer and ask if you wouldn't mind if you contact them on their behalf. When they say yes, collect their contact information and begin contacting them. Those referrals lead to new business as well, but the thing to remember and consider is this – you did nothing to attract this prospect into your business! Make sure that you are keeping track of the outcome of your appointments, so that you know our closing rate at all times. This will inform you on the effectiveness of your offer, salespeople and allow you to plan your future marketing efforts.

The rewards of 50Xing your company

If you decide to grow your business through networking, it is important, like anything else to be intentional with your efforts and focused on the desired outcomes. Otherwise, what you will find that networking is a complete waste of time. Yes, I said it! Networking is a complete waste of time without being purposeful and focused.

For best results, plan on attending every live Co-Op Network event and taking advantage of the opportunities we create for you to build alliances quickly. It is our goal of getting you and everyone else to the point to where you have at least 10 alliances consistently promoting your company. For those of you that build 50 plus alliances, you will be honored and recognized with a very special award and opportunities as a result. But most importantly, you will accelerate the growth of your company. The key to steady growth is to develop a lead generation machine that creates predictable, repeatable cash flow and Co-Opvertising™ is the key to making that happen!

CHAPTER NINE

TRACKING YOUR CO-OPVERTISING™ ACTIVITY

·····································

"What gets measured, gets done." – Jeff Levin

How many times have you invested in a seminar or conference, or attended a networking event & returned home charged with optimism and positive energy to tackle the world? How many have lost that energy a few days later and slumped back into your normal patterned behavior? I would say a good majority of you have. So isn't the point of attending events and learning new things to teach you how to do things differently going forward? Then what happened? There are many reasons why this may have occurred in your past, but one surefire way to ensure that something good happens is to follow a program and track your results.

In the appendix, we have provided you with the Co-Op Movement Goal and Activity Tracker designed to get you results through, focused, intentional, daily discipline. It takes discipline to achieve consistent results in anything in life and it will require discipline if you want to 50X your promotional power through the Co-Opvertising™ Network.

Here's a summary on how to use this simple tracker and what to do with it. If you follow the program correctly, we guarantee you will build a significant amount of momentum in your business and maximize the opportunities that are found by partnering with the people you meet in your networking efforts within participating Co-Opvertising™ Networks, both online and offline.

Getting Started

To get started, complete the Co-Opvertising™ Movement Goal Tracker on Day One! This will help you clarify what your expectations are within the Co-Opvertising™ Network & set your focus appropriately to achieve it.

After completing your Goal Tracker, all you have to do is review your goal tracker each day and complete the Daily Co-Opvertising™ Movement Tracker to summarize your activity for that day that moved you closer to reaching your goals.

If you happen to be confused where to begin, here's a checklist that I recommend following to get you off the ground running:

1. Determine Your Co-Opvertising™ Offer
2. Schedule Initial Meetings with the people you recently met at a Co-Opvertising™ Network Live Event or on the online forum to determine how to help them.
3. To help people first, promote the people you are meeting in the online Facebook group, which they will appreciate.
4. Schedule a follow-up meeting to present your Co-Op

Offer to determine if they would be willing to share your offer with their clients as a gift to their clients. A great way to get them to promote you, is to offer to promote them first in your Co-Op e-Newsletter via GrowthPOD.com.

5. If you have other ways to refer them business, by all means exchange referrals with the person and be sure to note it on your tracker.

6. Complete your daily Co-Op Movement Tracker to keep you focused on track to LevelUp your connections and LevelUp Your Business.

7. At the end of 30 days, complete your 30 Day Co-Opvertisng Movement Results Tracking Sheet and send it to results@Co-Opvertising™network.com to allow us to better connect, reward and recognize you for all of your accomplishments.

8. Continue to track your activity daily and submit your results every 30 days to grow.

By following these simple steps you will build strategic referral partners faster than ever before. I have personally built 60 active referral sources in 60 days using the methods that we are showing you right here and you can too.

How would your business and life look if you had 30 times the number active alliances you have right now promoting and referring you business on a consistent basis? Is it worth the discipline to help at least 1-2 people per day for a month and track your results? Of course it is and we look forward to celebrating your results with you in 30 days. By all means, if you find a reason to celebrate earlier, feel free to post to the Facebook group or email us at the address above any time and allow us to share in your progress. We are here to create the habits that breed long term success patterns and this is a major reason why you will be successful on our programs.

CHAPTER TEN

LEVELING UP YOUR BUSINESS

. . . .

"Your investment returns when others can benefit from what you've worked hard to build." – Jeff Levin

Before beginning this section, let me first say that there is no choice but to build a consistent repeatable cash machine in your business. By not doing this, you are virtually guaranteeing a long, hard road to survival in business, i.e., barely getting by. Consistency is key to growth and longevity in business, so everything we are speaking to in this book, if implemented will jump start the growth in your company if implemented correctly. In fact, we have built more than 60 alliances in less than 60 days several times and you can too, by following the system.

So, based upon what you have learned so far, will you go for it and build a promotional army or will you chalk this up to learning something new and move on? We did not invent the concept of partnering or strategic relationships – it has been around for many, many years and has always been a key reason why companies succeed long term. So if you can't do this to grow, then what shall you do? I would suggest going for it!

The LevelUp Business Growth Model

Co-Opvertising™ will kick your business into growth mode and do it quite quickly. So before, we go too far, lets' review the 4 stages of growth every company and entrepreneur goes through in order to build a business that is profitable and works, so you don't have to so much. Because at the end of the day, you are building a company, not a job. Think about the amount of time and energy you put into simply running your company. What would make that worthwhile? When you get your time and money back and then some right? So, it is my goal to help you realize that right now, from the beginning and get you focused on the end game, so that your time quickly becomes an investment, because your return comes when others can benefit from what you've built. I always say, you are building a prototype, so what is yours? What does your business need to look like in order to be attractive for others to come work for you? What does it need to look like in order for others to purchase a license or a franchise? These are all questions that should be answered upfront, so that every minute you invest in your company is done with the intent to build and grow it - grow it to the point where your prototype is lucrative enough for yourself and attractive enough for others to invest in .So what we are going to do is briefly walk through the different stages of entrepreneurship and company growth. As you are reading, ask yourself where do you fit right now and where and when do you wish to be there by? It will take focus, dedication and investment in yourself to grow both as a business and an entrepreneur.

THE LEVELUP GROWTH MODEL

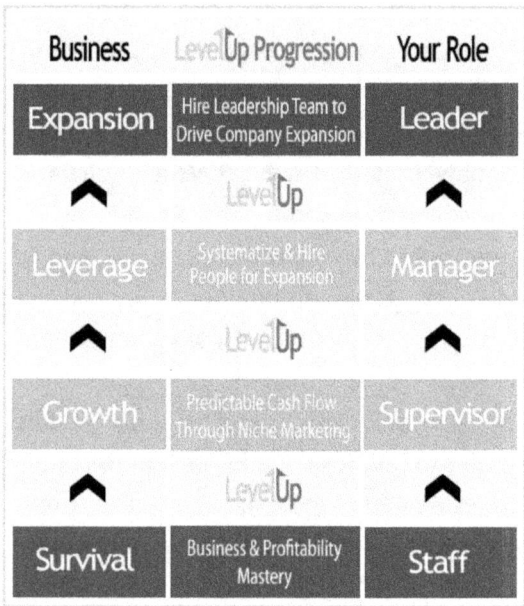

VISIT WWW.LEVELUPMYBIZ.COM AND TAKE THE FREE QUIZ TO SEE WHAT STAGE OF GROWTH YOU ARE IN NOW!

LevelUp Stage: Survival

Goal: Business & Profitability Mastery

Role: Staff Member

When we first go into business, the owners are usually handling nearly every role in the company. They answer the phones, build their websites, handle the sales, deliver the services or build the products, deposit checks, support the customers, market the business and then some. This is good because as a new entrepreneur, it is your job to learn your business and master it, so that you can one day delegate the responsibility to another person you hire or outsource for your company. However, what most fail to do during this timeframe is to define performance expectations so that you can define roles in your company and setup performance standards for others to uphold the qualify and efficiencies that your clientele have grown to expect. They don't do this quite frankly because they have yet to master the business themselves yet.

The goal of this stage is not only to master your business from an operational standpoint, but also from a profitability standpoint. To me, the fundamental way to have mastered your business is to become profitable! So companies exit the survival stage of business when they know and understand their numbers. We highly encourage you to visit www.levelupmybiz.com to determine your break-even profitability to learn our 5 growth Key Performance Metrics every company needs to know to grow their companies.

LevelUp Stage: Growth

Goal: Predictable Cash Flow

Role: Supervisor

So, after you have reached the break-even point in business, the goal is to continue to grow and become more profitable. At some point you will reach maximum capacity for the amount of work you can physically do on your own, because you are growing, so you need a consistent, repeatable cash flow model that will enable you to hire people to serve in different roles within the company and at the same time, be able to pay them. Companies in the Growth stage have carved a niche typically and are achieving high levels of customer service. They also have taken the leap to hire someone to level up their role in the business to a Supervisor role. Take the business survival quiz right now at www.levelupmybiz.com to see if what stage of growth you are in.

LevelUp Stage: Leverage

Goal: Systematize and Hire People for Expansion

Role: Manager

My rule of thumb is to systematize the routine and humanize the exceptions. So after you have learned how your business operates in the Survival Stage, it's time to begin building systems and process into your company then determining whether to hire or automate the function. In this role, you have Leveled Up to a Manager role in your company. Take the business survival quiz right now at www.levelupmybiz.com to see if what stage of growth you are in.

LevelUp Stage: Expansion

Goal: To Exit Core Operations of the Company and Hire Leadership to Expand and Grow

Role: CEO/Company Leader

As we mentioned earlier, you are building a business and the first location is your prototype. After you've built the first one that has become profitable and suitable for your own needs, then there is now an opportunity to package your prototype in a way to attract investors, partners, licensees, buyers and even employees. So even in the beginning, it is important to know what you are building! I'm sure you have heard the term scalability, well this level is where your business becomes scalable and it is also where you begin to see the return on your investment. In my opinion, you need to have a vision for expansion and understand how it will work best for your company early on. So if you don't have the vision or see how expansion will work, now is the time to sit down and find it. How will you serve the masses by staying small? It's time to expand your vision to complete your mission.

We hope this has stimulated a new vision and thought process for how you will proceed in the growth and development of yourself and your business. We do this because, we need your company to grow and serve the masses. We need you to employ people. We need you to be extremely profitable so that you can give people hope and a sense of belonging in the communities you live and operate within. To see where you stand in your business growth, visit www.levelupmybiz.com now to take our free quiz.

We hope this book has opened your eyes to the new and exciting possibilities of building a business to serve the masses. It is my life's work and ambition to provide the channels to assist you in finding your true gifts and giving you the platform and strategies to share that gift with the world. Only when you decide to do so, will you unlock your true potential. This message can change so many lives, but we cannot do this without your help. So if you received value from this book, please consider sponsoring the Co-Op Movement now at www.Co-Opvertisingnetwork.com/sponsorship and think about how best you can help us share our mission with the world. Thank you so much! Now get out there and lead with your mission, serve the masses and become massively successful!

CHAPTER ELEVEN

JOINING THE CO-OPVERTISING™ MOVEMENT

••••••••••••••••••••••••••••••••

"Have Purpose for Your Profits." – Jeff Levin

A wise person once told me that you will be as good as the people you surround yourself with. So if you want to LevelUp your business, you probably want to be around people that are on mission for something more and are heavily committed to building their companies to serve the masses. That's the kind of environment we have built in the Chicagoland area and it is our goal to take this prototype that we've built across the United States. And the cool part about this, is you have the ability to attend, grow and prosper wherever we have events and Co-Opvertising™ Networks and at some levels, you get to do it FREE.

When we first began the Co-Op Movement, I decided to not call our members, but instead call them sponsors because I wanted to create a greater sense of ownership amongst the people of the community. I wanted our people to be the fuel that allows us to push out our mission of re-defining success all across the county and the only way to do that is from the support of our sponsors. Now, similar to the crowd funding model, the more our sponsors give and contribute, the more perks they get. So for some levels you will get to attend events free at any location. At higher levels, you not only get to attend events free, but you also get recognition at the events and even further, you get access to coaching and more! To succeed this way, you have to have a giving mentality and our business model is structured to attract the people that get it. And as you can probably suspect, the people that sponsor at the highest levels, most definitely get the most out of our environment! So, we encourage you to sponsor the movement and help us reach more and more people across this country. Visit www.Co-Opvertisingnetwork.com/sponsorship to learn more about the different levels of sponsorship.

You can also join us online free on Facebook by searching for Co-Opvertising™ Network. You will find several Facebook groups in the results. Please feel free to join and add your friends in business that you feel would be excellent additions to the movement and together we can reach the 28 million entrepreneurs across the U.S.

We also host an online, Facebook Live Daily Talk Show we call "Co-Opie Talk", broadcasted live at 9am central every week day. Each day we talk about different topics associated with being in business and highlight companies in the Co-Op Network. If you would like to be a guest on the show, visit www.Co-Opvertisingnetwork.com/coopietalk today and request to be on the show to join the conversation and let us help you promote your business. To watch previous shows and receive notifications when we go live, like us on Facebook @coopietalk now and share out the page to your Entrepreneur friends.

Bring the Co-Op Movement to You

We are looking for leaders in cities across the United States to bring the Co-Op Movement to their cities. I was taught long ago that there is nothing more powerful in achieving long term success in business, that building and leading a network. If you consider yourself to be a charismatic leader that wishes to not only be a part of something great, but also establish yourself as a leader in your industry and community, then we want to speak with you! Contact us today at (866) 217-8425. Through this process we will teach you how to build a network and consistently attract hundreds to our events! This opportunity is limited to one partner per major city and includes the opportunity to monetize your network building activities. Contact us today!

ABOUT THE AUTHOR

Jeff Levin is driven to help you unlock your true purpose, gifts and talents that God has given to every person on the planet.

✓ He is an expert in Guerrilla Marketing, having developed highly leveraged marketing and networking platforms that allow entrepreneurs to create massive leverage in their businesses, at little to no costs.
✓ He has built million dollar franchiseable companies as a business builder.
✓ He has built one of the fastest growing entrepreneurial networks in the Chicagoland Area that has attracted some of the most sought after, influential speakers in the world to speak from his stages at the Co-Op Movement Live Events packed with hundreds of Entrepreneurs excited about his mission.
✓ He is a devout Christian that believes when you are willing to serve the masses with your gifts you will become massively successful. And as a bonus, when you choose to do it for God, you will experience successes beyond your wildest dreams.

He believes with conviction that Entrepreneurs are the most influential and impactful people on the planet, because they have to be. It is Jeff's goal to reach every Entrepreneur on the planet through his books, live events, shows and partnerships and together help re-define what success is all about, because he believes a company with purpose, will not only be extremely successful, but will also change the world! If you would like to help us reach the 28 million Entrepreneurs across the country, by bringing him into speak or offering the ability to facilitate a Co-Opvertising™ Live Event in your area, contact him today at (866) 217-8425.

JEFF LEVIN

APPENDIX A

CO-OPVERTISING™ EXAMPLES

....

1. Video Production Company

Give away a Free Intro for self made videos with a goal of producing a professional promotional video.

2. Marketing Company

Give away a FREE logo design with a goal of producing the marketing materials to use the logo on.

3. Accounting Company

Give away QuickBooks Training with the goal of landing clients for financial management, tax planning and bookkeeping. Great way to partner with others in the bookkeeping industry.

4. Construction Company/Home Remodeling Co.

Free Handyman Services with the goal of landing home projects and remodeling.

5. Direct Sales Clothing Retailer for Women

Fashion Show for Clients of High Traffic Salons

6. Professional Organizer

1 hour of FREE organizing something specific like a desk or a

closet.

7. Marketing/Branding Co.

FREE logo design

8. Chiropractor/Wellness Co.

FREE Groceries to Realtor Clients

9. Travel Agent

Provide FREE inspirational framed photos to the audiences of success/business coaches (because their job is to give their clients more life)

10. Business Coaching Company

FREE seminars (valuable info products) delivered for clients of B-B businesses

11. Wedding Cake Company

Offer a FREE Shower Cake for photographers, florists and other wedding service providers to give away to their clients when they purchase their products.

12. Financial Planner

Offer to put on FREE educational events or programs for children around investments and money and partner with companies that have access to kids.

13. Printer

Offer free business card design or logo design and partner with business to business companies.

14. Insurance Agent

The whole point of Co-Opvertising™ is to drive traffic to your business, so this business would be best to have FREE giveaways that people want like movie tickets, car washes, massages, cleaning services etc, but the idea would be to get these companies to give them to you to give away.

15. Photographer

Give away a free social media headshot in hopes to sell high quality digital and printed images.

16. Realtor

The point of Co-Opvertising™ is to drive traffic. So what I would do is approach contractors that can help not only prep homes for sale, but also help new home owners settle in with customizations. Coach your contractors how to package what they do as a gift for others to share and then give it away to your prospective home buyers as a package deal. So you can put together a download or a video that includes Your 7 Secrets you use to sell homes in under 30 days. Then in the download offer a free in person home assessment to put your plan together to sell and for booking, give them over $5000 in real value (provided from your contractors)

17. Interior Designer

Offer a FREE training course on how to decorate your home and give it to realtors and other contractors to give away. Inside the video or trainings, you should sell your services and make an offer for them signing up right away.

18. Personality Tests

Offer anyone in the business of closing sales a FREE training on how to sell to different personality types and approach companies with business clients to put on a live training or webinar specific for their business.

19. Banks

Offer FREE business training course delivered by local business experts then approach local business experts and ask if they can deliver the workshops in exchange for the opportunity to position their services.

20. Hair Stylist

Give FREE Hair Cuts to any business. Or approach youth sports organizations and as the kids sell raffle tickets, they can give the purchase a coupon for a FREE haircut, which will keep the value and also help the cause.

21. Sports Clubs

Team with companies that target kids and parents and provide FREE clinics or trainings for their kids.

22. Credit Card Processing

Bring value to Business to Business companies that attract high traffic. For example, partner with an organization like the Co-Op Network and give us packaged value you've arranged from your business alliances, in exchange for making an offer from stage, having an offer on the feedback form or the ability to do a direct email blast following the event. The key is to bring value the organization can give away.

23. HVAC company

Partner with Insurance Agents and give them your annual maintenance program free to give away to their clients.

24. Cleaning Company

Give Realtors and any other companies that deal with the interior of the home a FREE home cleaning.

25. Landscapers

FREE lawn cut by partnering with companies that do nothing but mowing and maintenance.

26. Landscape Lighting

Offer 1 Free Maintenance call or outdoor lighting demonstration and give it to high end home service providers like landscapers, pool companies, irrigation companies, etc.

27. Roofer

Offer FREE hail damage assessment that could be covered up to 100% and give this to alliances that service high end homeowners. Gather or purchase VIP tickets to parade of homes in your area, and give them to your home service alliances to give to their clients but they must be redeemed through you (the roofer)

28. Painter

Offer a FREE accent wall to alliances that service homeowners.

29. Graphic Designer

Offer 1 FREE social media ad design or a "do it yourself" e-book or video on how to design a marketing piece.

30. Dog Walker

Offer 1 FREE pet sitting session and partner with cleaning services and other high end home service providers.

31. Lawn Maintenance

Offer 1 FREE mowing and work with realtors, cleaning services and other companies that gain access to new residents moving into neighborhoods.

32. Life Coach

Build a FREE webinar or e-series for your target market and the give it to alliances that share a similar interest.

33. Yoga company

Offer a FREE 30 day membership for your alliances to give away.

34. Appliance Repair Company

Offer a DIY Guide or Video Series on How to Fix common appliance issues in the home and give it alliances that deal with home owners.

35. Personal Trainer

Offer a FREE DIY weight loss program with 1 FREE personal training session and give it to any alliance you form that wants to promote health and wellness.

36. Coffee Company

Offer a FREE bag of specialty coffee for alliances to give their clients as a gift.

37. Copywriter

Offer to write 1 FREE blog or facebook post for B-B Alliances.

38. Virtual Assistant

Offer 3 FREE hours of virtual assistant work

39. Attorney

Offer 1 FREE contract review

40. Event Planner

Offer a FREE Downloadable DIY Wedding Planner Guide. You can also sign up for a Bridal show and then partner with several wedding service providers to do a drawing for a FREE wedding. This will attract several entries into your drawing for follow-up and closure for the people that do not win. Your alliances will want to do this because they will want access to the marketing list and opportunities closed from the event planner.

41. Catering Company

Offer FREE catering for a party for the rehearsal dinner and give this to your wedding alliance vendors. The goal would be to sell catering services for the wedding.

APPENDIX B.
THE CO-OPVERTISING™ MOVEMENT GOAL SETTER
30 DAYS TO ACTIVE ALLIANCES
(TO BE COMPLETED ON DAY ONE)

....

DAY 1 SUMMARY (DATE): _____

CO-OPVERTISING™

OFFER:_____

ACQUISITION COST:

_____

LIFETIME VALUE OF A CUSTOMER: _____

TARGET MARKET: _____

BUSINESS CATEGORIES THAT TARGET THE SAME MARKET:

CURRENT TOTAL ACTIVE ALLIANCES: _____

I WOULD LIKE TO INCREASE MY ACTIVE ALLIANCES AND
PROMOTIONAL PARTNERS OVER THE NEXT 30 DAYS BY:
5X_____ 10X_____ 20X_____30X_____40X_____50X_____

HOW MANY PEOPLE WOULD YOU BE IN FRONT OF IF YOU BUILT
MORE ALLIANCES:

_____

YOUR FOLLOWING STATISTICS:
EMAIL DATABASE SIZE: _____FACEBOOK FRIENDS: _____
TWITTER FOLLOWERS: _____LINKEDIN:_____
INSTAGRAM: _____GROWTHPOD: _____

GOAL NO. OF CO-OPVERTISING™ CAMPAIGNS SENT THAT
INCLUDES YOUR CO-OP OFFER:_____

REFERRAL GOAL:_____ EXPOSURE GOAL: _____

GOAL OF REVENUE GENERATED FROM ALLIANCES: _____

THE DAILY CO-OPVERTISING™ MOVEMENT TRACKER
30 DAYS TO ACTIVE ALLIANCES

DAY 1:
MEETINGS SCHEDULED:_____ MEETINGS HELD:_____
NUMBER OF POSTS HELPING OTHERS: _____
REFERRALS RECEIVED: _____ REFERRALS GIVEN: _____
TOTAL ACTIVE ALLIANCES (PEOPLE PROMOTING YOU OR SCHEDULED
TO PROMOTE YOU THIS MONTH): _____
REVENUE GENERATED FROM REFERRALS AND ALLIANCES: _____
COMMENTS/THOUGHTS ON THE OUTCOME OF HELPING OTHERS
TODAY?

DAY 2:
MEETINGS SCHEDULED:_____ MEETINGS HELD:_____
NUMBER OF POSTS HELPING OTHERS: _____
REFERRALS RECEIVED: _____ REFERRALS GIVEN: _____
TOTAL ACTIVE ALLIANCES (PEOPLE PROMOTING YOU OR SCHEDULED
TO PROMOTE YOU THIS MONTH): _____
REVENUE GENERATED FROM REFERRALS AND ALLIANCES: _____
COMMENTS/THOUGHTS ON THE OUTCOME OF HELPING OTHERS
TODAY?

DAY 3:
MEETINGS SCHEDULED:_____ MEETINGS HELD:_____
NUMBER OF POSTS HELPING OTHERS: _____
REFERRALS RECEIVED: _____ REFERRALS GIVEN: _____
TOTAL ACTIVE ALLIANCES (PEOPLE PROMOTING YOU OR SCHEDULED
TO PROMOTE YOU THIS MONTH): _____
REVENUE GENERATED FROM REFERRALS AND ALLIANCES: _____
COMMENTS/THOUGHTS ON THE OUTCOME OF HELPING OTHERS
TODAY?

THE DAILY CO-OPVERTISING™ MOVEMENT TRACKER
30 DAYS TO ACTIVE ALLIANCES

DAY 4:
MEETINGS SCHEDULED:____ MEETINGS HELD:_____
NUMBER OF POSTS HELPING OTHERS: _____
REFERRALS RECEIVED: _____ REFERRALS GIVEN: _____
TOTAL ACTIVE ALLIANCES (PEOPLE PROMOTING YOU OR SCHEDULED
TO PROMOTE YOU THIS MONTH): _____
REVENUE GENERATED FROM REFERRALS AND ALLIANCES: _____
COMMENTS/THOUGHTS ON THE OUTCOME OF HELPING OTHERS
TODAY?

DAY 5:
MEETINGS SCHEDULED:____ MEETINGS HELD:_____
NUMBER OF POSTS HELPING OTHERS: _____
REFERRALS RECEIVED: _____ REFERRALS GIVEN: _____
TOTAL ACTIVE ALLIANCES (PEOPLE PROMOTING YOU OR SCHEDULED
TO PROMOTE YOU THIS MONTH): _____
REVENUE GENERATED FROM REFERRALS AND ALLIANCES: _____
COMMENTS/THOUGHTS ON THE OUTCOME OF HELPING OTHERS
TODAY?

DAY 6:
MEETINGS SCHEDULED:____ MEETINGS HELD:_____
NUMBER OF POSTS HELPING OTHERS: _____
REFERRALS RECEIVED: _____ REFERRALS GIVEN: _____
TOTAL ACTIVE ALLIANCES (PEOPLE PROMOTING YOU OR SCHEDULED
TO PROMOTE YOU THIS MONTH): _____
REVENUE GENERATED FROM REFERRALS AND ALLIANCES: _____
COMMENTS/THOUGHTS ON THE OUTCOME OF HELPING OTHERS
TODAY?

THE DAILY CO-OPVERTISING™ MOVEMENT TRACKER
30 DAYS TO ACTIVE ALLIANCES

DAY 7:
MEETINGS SCHEDULED:_____ MEETINGS HELD:_____
NUMBER OF POSTS HELPING OTHERS: _____
REFERRALS RECEIVED: _____ REFERRALS GIVEN: _____
TOTAL ACTIVE ALLIANCES (PEOPLE PROMOTING YOU OR SCHEDULED
TO PROMOTE YOU THIS MONTH): _____
REVENUE GENERATED FROM REFERRALS AND ALLIANCES: _____
COMMENTS/THOUGHTS ON THE OUTCOME OF HELPING OTHERS
TODAY?

DAY 8:
MEETINGS SCHEDULED:_____ MEETINGS HELD:_____
NUMBER OF POSTS HELPING OTHERS: _____
REFERRALS RECEIVED: _____ REFERRALS GIVEN: _____
TOTAL ACTIVE ALLIANCES (PEOPLE PROMOTING YOU OR SCHEDULED
TO PROMOTE YOU THIS MONTH): _____
REVENUE GENERATED FROM REFERRALS AND ALLIANCES: _____
COMMENTS/THOUGHTS ON THE OUTCOME OF HELPING OTHERS
TODAY?

DAY 9:
MEETINGS SCHEDULED:_____ MEETINGS HELD:_____
NUMBER OF POSTS HELPING OTHERS: _____
REFERRALS RECEIVED: _____ REFERRALS GIVEN: _____
TOTAL ACTIVE ALLIANCES (PEOPLE PROMOTING YOU OR SCHEDULED
TO PROMOTE YOU THIS MONTH): _____
REVENUE GENERATED FROM REFERRALS AND ALLIANCES: _____
COMMENTS/THOUGHTS ON THE OUTCOME OF HELPING OTHERS
TODAY?

THE DAILY CO-OPVERTISING™ MOVEMENT TRACKER
30 DAYS TO ACTIVE ALLIANCES

DAY 10:
MEETINGS SCHEDULED:_____ MEETINGS HELD:_____
NUMBER OF POSTS HELPING OTHERS: _____
REFERRALS RECEIVED: _____ REFERRALS GIVEN: _____
TOTAL ACTIVE ALLIANCES (PEOPLE PROMOTING YOU OR SCHEDULED
TO PROMOTE YOU THIS MONTH): _____
REVENUE GENERATED FROM REFERRALS AND ALLIANCES: _____
COMMENTS/THOUGHTS ON THE OUTCOME OF HELPING OTHERS
TODAY?

DAY 11:
MEETINGS SCHEDULED:_____ MEETINGS HELD:_____
NUMBER OF POSTS HELPING OTHERS: _____
REFERRALS RECEIVED: _____ REFERRALS GIVEN: _____
TOTAL ACTIVE ALLIANCES (PEOPLE PROMOTING YOU OR SCHEDULED
TO PROMOTE YOU THIS MONTH): _____
REVENUE GENERATED FROM REFERRALS AND ALLIANCES: _____
COMMENTS/THOUGHTS ON THE OUTCOME OF HELPING OTHERS
TODAY?

DAY 12:
MEETINGS SCHEDULED:_____ MEETINGS HELD:_____
NUMBER OF POSTS HELPING OTHERS: _____
REFERRALS RECEIVED: _____ REFERRALS GIVEN: _____
TOTAL ACTIVE ALLIANCES (PEOPLE PROMOTING YOU OR SCHEDULED
TO PROMOTE YOU THIS MONTH): _____
REVENUE GENERATED FROM REFERRALS AND ALLIANCES: _____
COMMENTS/THOUGHTS ON THE OUTCOME OF HELPING OTHERS
TODAY?

THE DAILY CO-OPVERTISING™ MOVEMENT TRACKER
30 DAYS TO ACTIVE ALLIANCES

DAY 13:
MEETINGS SCHEDULED:_____ MEETINGS HELD:_____
NUMBER OF POSTS HELPING OTHERS: _____
REFERRALS RECEIVED: _____ REFERRALS GIVEN: _____
TOTAL ACTIVE ALLIANCES (PEOPLE PROMOTING YOU OR SCHEDULED
TO PROMOTE YOU THIS MONTH): _____
REVENUE GENERATED FROM REFERRALS AND ALLIANCES: _____
COMMENTS/THOUGHTS ON THE OUTCOME OF HELPING OTHERS
TODAY?

DAY 14:
MEETINGS SCHEDULED:_____ MEETINGS HELD:_____
NUMBER OF POSTS HELPING OTHERS: _____
REFERRALS RECEIVED: _____ REFERRALS GIVEN: _____
TOTAL ACTIVE ALLIANCES (PEOPLE PROMOTING YOU OR SCHEDULED
TO PROMOTE YOU THIS MONTH): _____
REVENUE GENERATED FROM REFERRALS AND ALLIANCES: _____
COMMENTS/THOUGHTS ON THE OUTCOME OF HELPING OTHERS
TODAY?

DAY 15:
MEETINGS SCHEDULED:_____ MEETINGS HELD:_____
NUMBER OF POSTS HELPING OTHERS: _____
REFERRALS RECEIVED: _____ REFERRALS GIVEN: _____
TOTAL ACTIVE ALLIANCES (PEOPLE PROMOTING YOU OR SCHEDULED
TO PROMOTE YOU THIS MONTH): _____
REVENUE GENERATED FROM REFERRALS AND ALLIANCES: _____
COMMENTS/THOUGHTS ON THE OUTCOME OF HELPING OTHERS
TODAY?

THE DAILY CO-OPVERTISING™ MOVEMENT TRACKER
30 DAYS TO ACTIVE ALLIANCES

DAY 16:
MEETINGS SCHEDULED:_____ MEETINGS HELD:_____
NUMBER OF POSTS HELPING OTHERS: _____
REFERRALS RECEIVED: _____ REFERRALS GIVEN: _____
TOTAL ACTIVE ALLIANCES (PEOPLE PROMOTING YOU OR SCHEDULED
TO PROMOTE YOU THIS MONTH): _____
REVENUE GENERATED FROM REFERRALS AND ALLIANCES: _____
COMMENTS/THOUGHTS ON THE OUTCOME OF HELPING OTHERS
TODAY?

DAY 17:
MEETINGS SCHEDULED:_____ MEETINGS HELD:_____
NUMBER OF POSTS HELPING OTHERS: _____
REFERRALS RECEIVED: _____ REFERRALS GIVEN: _____
TOTAL ACTIVE ALLIANCES (PEOPLE PROMOTING YOU OR SCHEDULED
TO PROMOTE YOU THIS MONTH): _____
REVENUE GENERATED FROM REFERRALS AND ALLIANCES: _____
COMMENTS/THOUGHTS ON THE OUTCOME OF HELPING OTHERS
TODAY?

DAY 18:
MEETINGS SCHEDULED:_____ MEETINGS HELD:_____
NUMBER OF POSTS HELPING OTHERS: _____
REFERRALS RECEIVED: _____ REFERRALS GIVEN: _____
TOTAL ACTIVE ALLIANCES (PEOPLE PROMOTING YOU OR SCHEDULED
TO PROMOTE YOU THIS MONTH): _____
REVENUE GENERATED FROM REFERRALS AND ALLIANCES: _____
COMMENTS/THOUGHTS ON THE OUTCOME OF HELPING OTHERS
TODAY?

THE DAILY CO-OPVERTISING™ MOVEMENT TRACKER
30 DAYS TO ACTIVE ALLIANCES

DAY 19:
MEETINGS SCHEDULED:____ MEETINGS HELD:_____
NUMBER OF POSTS HELPING OTHERS: _____
REFERRALS RECEIVED: _____ REFERRALS GIVEN: _____
TOTAL ACTIVE ALLIANCES (PEOPLE PROMOTING YOU OR SCHEDULED
TO PROMOTE YOU THIS MONTH): _____
REVENUE GENERATED FROM REFERRALS AND ALLIANCES: _____
COMMENTS/THOUGHTS ON THE OUTCOME OF HELPING OTHERS
TODAY?

DAY 20:
MEETINGS SCHEDULED:____ MEETINGS HELD:_____
NUMBER OF POSTS HELPING OTHERS: _____
REFERRALS RECEIVED: _____ REFERRALS GIVEN: _____
TOTAL ACTIVE ALLIANCES (PEOPLE PROMOTING YOU OR SCHEDULED
TO PROMOTE YOU THIS MONTH): _____
REVENUE GENERATED FROM REFERRALS AND ALLIANCES: _____
COMMENTS/THOUGHTS ON THE OUTCOME OF HELPING OTHERS
TODAY?

DAY 21:
MEETINGS SCHEDULED:____ MEETINGS HELD:_____
NUMBER OF POSTS HELPING OTHERS: _____
REFERRALS RECEIVED: _____ REFERRALS GIVEN: _____
TOTAL ACTIVE ALLIANCES (PEOPLE PROMOTING YOU OR SCHEDULED
TO PROMOTE YOU THIS MONTH): _____
REVENUE GENERATED FROM REFERRALS AND ALLIANCES: _____
COMMENTS/THOUGHTS ON THE OUTCOME OF HELPING OTHERS
TODAY?

THE DAILY CO-OPVERTISING™ MOVEMENT TRACKER
30 DAYS TO ACTIVE ALLIANCES

DAY 22:
MEETINGS SCHEDULED:____ MEETINGS HELD:_____
NUMBER OF POSTS HELPING OTHERS: _____
REFERRALS RECEIVED: _____ REFERRALS GIVEN: _____
TOTAL ACTIVE ALLIANCES (PEOPLE PROMOTING YOU OR SCHEDULED
TO PROMOTE YOU THIS MONTH): _____
REVENUE GENERATED FROM REFERRALS AND ALLIANCES: _____
COMMENTS/THOUGHTS ON THE OUTCOME OF HELPING OTHERS
TODAY?

DAY 23:
MEETINGS SCHEDULED:____ MEETINGS HELD:_____
NUMBER OF POSTS HELPING OTHERS: _____
REFERRALS RECEIVED: _____ REFERRALS GIVEN: _____
TOTAL ACTIVE ALLIANCES (PEOPLE PROMOTING YOU OR SCHEDULED
TO PROMOTE YOU THIS MONTH): _____
REVENUE GENERATED FROM REFERRALS AND ALLIANCES: _____
COMMENTS/THOUGHTS ON THE OUTCOME OF HELPING OTHERS
TODAY?

DAY 24:
MEETINGS SCHEDULED:____ MEETINGS HELD:_____
NUMBER OF POSTS HELPING OTHERS: _____
REFERRALS RECEIVED: _____ REFERRALS GIVEN: _____
TOTAL ACTIVE ALLIANCES (PEOPLE PROMOTING YOU OR SCHEDULED
TO PROMOTE YOU THIS MONTH): _____
REVENUE GENERATED FROM REFERRALS AND ALLIANCES: _____
COMMENTS/THOUGHTS ON THE OUTCOME OF HELPING OTHERS
TODAY?

THE DAILY CO-OPVERTISING™ MOVEMENT TRACKER
30 DAYS TO ACTIVE ALLIANCES

DAY 25:
MEETINGS SCHEDULED:_____ MEETINGS HELD:_____
NUMBER OF POSTS HELPING OTHERS: _____
REFERRALS RECEIVED: _____ REFERRALS GIVEN: _____
TOTAL ACTIVE ALLIANCES (PEOPLE PROMOTING YOU OR SCHEDULED
TO PROMOTE YOU THIS MONTH): _____
REVENUE GENERATED FROM REFERRALS AND ALLIANCES: _____
COMMENTS/THOUGHTS ON THE OUTCOME OF HELPING OTHERS
TODAY?

DAY 26:
MEETINGS SCHEDULED:_____ MEETINGS HELD:_____
NUMBER OF POSTS HELPING OTHERS: _____
REFERRALS RECEIVED: _____ REFERRALS GIVEN: _____
TOTAL ACTIVE ALLIANCES (PEOPLE PROMOTING YOU OR SCHEDULED
TO PROMOTE YOU THIS MONTH): _____
REVENUE GENERATED FROM REFERRALS AND ALLIANCES: _____
COMMENTS/THOUGHTS ON THE OUTCOME OF HELPING OTHERS
TODAY?

DAY 27:
MEETINGS SCHEDULED:_____ MEETINGS HELD:_____
NUMBER OF POSTS HELPING OTHERS: _____
REFERRALS RECEIVED: _____ REFERRALS GIVEN: _____
TOTAL ACTIVE ALLIANCES (PEOPLE PROMOTING YOU OR SCHEDULED
TO PROMOTE YOU THIS MONTH): _____
REVENUE GENERATED FROM REFERRALS AND ALLIANCES: _____
COMMENTS/THOUGHTS ON THE OUTCOME OF HELPING OTHERS
TODAY?

THE DAILY CO-OPVERTISING™ MOVEMENT TRACKER
30 DAYS TO ACTIVE ALLIANCES

DAY 28:
MEETINGS SCHEDULED:____ MEETINGS HELD:_____
NUMBER OF POSTS HELPING OTHERS: _____
REFERRALS RECEIVED: _____ REFERRALS GIVEN: _____
TOTAL ACTIVE ALLIANCES (PEOPLE PROMOTING YOU OR SCHEDULED
TO PROMOTE YOU THIS MONTH): _____
REVENUE GENERATED FROM REFERRALS AND ALLIANCES: _____
COMMENTS/THOUGHTS ON THE OUTCOME OF HELPING OTHERS
TODAY?

DAY 29:
MEETINGS SCHEDULED:____ MEETINGS HELD:_____
NUMBER OF POSTS HELPING OTHERS: _____
REFERRALS RECEIVED: _____ REFERRALS GIVEN: _____
TOTAL ACTIVE ALLIANCES (PEOPLE PROMOTING YOU OR SCHEDULED
TO PROMOTE YOU THIS MONTH): _____
REVENUE GENERATED FROM REFERRALS AND ALLIANCES: _____
COMMENTS/THOUGHTS ON THE OUTCOME OF HELPING OTHERS
TODAY?

DAY 30:
MEETINGS SCHEDULED:____ MEETINGS HELD:_____
NUMBER OF POSTS HELPING OTHERS: _____
REFERRALS RECEIVED: _____ REFERRALS GIVEN: _____
TOTAL ACTIVE ALLIANCES (PEOPLE PROMOTING YOU OR SCHEDULED
TO PROMOTE YOU THIS MONTH): _____
REVENUE GENERATED FROM REFERRALS AND ALLIANCES: _____
COMMENTS/THOUGHTS ON THE OUTCOME OF HELPING OTHERS
TODAY?

THE CO-OPVERTISING™ ALLIANCE TRACKER SUMMARY
30 DAYS TO ACTIVE ALLIANCES
(TO BE COMPLETED ON DAY 30)

DAY 30 SUMMARY (DATE): _____

CURRENT TOTAL ACTIVE ALLIANCES: _____

NO. OF CO-OPVERTISING™ CAMPAIGNS SENT THAT INCLUDED MY CO-OP OFFER: _____

TOTAL PROMOTIONAL EXPOSURE RECEIVED: _____

REFERRALS RECEIVED: _____ **REFERRALS GIVEN:** _____

REVENUE GENERATED: _____

OVER THE LAST 30 DAYS, I GREW MY ALLIANCES BY:

5X_____ 10X_____ 20X_____ 30X_____ 40X_____ 50X_____

YOUR FOLLOWING STATISTICS:

EMAIL DATABASE SIZE: _____FACEBOOK FRIENDS: _____

TWITTER FOLLOWERS: _____LINKEDIN:_____

INSTAGRAM: _____GROWTHPOD: _____

GOALS FOR THE NEXT 30 DAYS:

GOAL NO. OF CO-OPVERTISING™ CAMPAIGNS SENT THAT INCLUDES YOUR CO-OP OFFER:_____

REFERRAL GOAL:_____ EXPOSURE GOAL: _____

REVENUE GOAL FROM ALLIANCES & REFERRALS: _____

I WOULD LIKE TO INCREASE MY ACTIVE ALLIANCES AND PROMOTIONAL PARTNERS OVER THE NEXT 30 DAYS BY:

5X_____ 10X_____ 20X_____ 30X_____ 40X_____ 50X____

NAME: _____ BUSINESS CATEGORY:_____

CITY/STATE: _____ SPONSOR LEVEL: _____

REVENUE PAST 12 MONTHS: _____

REVENUE PAST MONTH: _____

PLEASE SCAN AND SEND EVERY MONTH TO RESULTS@CO-OPVERTISING™NETWORK.COM FOR REWARDS AND RECOGNITION ONLINE AND AT LIVE CO-OP EVENTS. YOUR RESULTS WILL REMAIN CONFIDENTIAL.

BOOK JEFF LEVIN TO SPEAK AT YOUR NEXT EVENT

....

Jeff Levin is a charismatic, influential and inspiring speaker that is available to share his message with your audience of independent sales professionals and entrepreneurs about a variety of topics including:

- ✓ **The Secret to LevelUp Your Business**
- ✓ **Lead with Your Mission & Your Business Will Follow**
- ✓ **How to 50X Your Business Through Co-Opvertising™**

In addition, if you run an organization of entrepreneurs, we would enjoy coming in to facilitate a Co-Opvertising™ Live Event for your organization. You provide the people, we will provide the program.

We have a limited number of available dates. Contact us today to setup this opportunity to become an official Co-Op Movement Network and be a part of helping us reach 28 million Entrepreneurs across this country with a new definition of success! Call (866) 217-8425.

LEVELUP YOUR BUSINESS

....

Jeff Levin has built million dollar franchiseable companies and worked with thousands of Entrepreneurs since 2003, when he became a business coach, to compliment his B.S. in Electrical Engineering and Masters in Business Administration (MBA). In addition to his programs, Jeff has worked alongside of leading Entrepreneurs in the Business Coaching & Success Community like Brad Sugars, Kurek Ashley, Loral Langemeier, Albert Mensah, Greg Reid, David Meltzer, David Sheffield, Johnny Campbell, Abby Kohut, Patrick Snow and Shelia Skolnick to offer Entrepreneurs programs to LevelUp their businesses. Now, Jeff is proud to offer a very special program of his own to his readers called **LevelUp Your Business – Survival Training.**

It's a 52 Week Program that shares the learnings via video and email guiding you through the exact steps, in the same sequence, he's used to accelerate the growth of hundreds of companies and build million dollar companies.

Visit www.levelupmybiz.com now!

SAVE 50%

using the code:

BOOKSPECIAL

www.ingramcontent.com/pod-product-compliance
Lightning Source LLC
Chambersburg PA
CBHW070041210526
45170CB00012B/562